SIXTH EDITION

INTERACTIONS
Reading

ACCESS

Pamela Hartmann

James Mentel

Mc
Graw
Hill

Interactions Access Reading, Sixth Edition

Published by McGraw-Hill ESL/ELT, a business unit of The McGraw-Hill Companies, Inc., 1221 Avenue of the Americas, New York, NY 10020. Copyright © 2014 by The McGraw-Hill Companies, Inc. All rights reserved. Printed in the United States of America. Previous editions © 2007, 2001, and 1995. No part of this publication may be reproduced or distributed in any form or by any means, or stored in a database or retrieval system, without the prior written consent of The McGraw-Hill Companies, Inc., including, but not limited to, in any network or other electronic storage or transmission, or broadcast for distance learning.

Some ancillaries, including electronic and print components, may not be available to customers outside the United States.

This book is printed on acid-free paper.

2 3 4 5 6 7 8 9 0 DOW/DOW 1 0 9 8 7 6 5 4 3

ISBN: 978-0-07-801963-0
MHID: 0-07-801963-X

Senior Vice President, Products & Markets: Kurt L. Strand
Vice President, General Manager, Products & Markets: Michael J. Ryan
Vice President, Content Production & Technology Services: Kimberly Meriwether David
Director of Development: Valerie Kelemen
Marketing Manager: Cambridge University Press
Lead Project Manager: Rick Hecker
Senior Buyer: Michael R. McCormick
Designer: Page2, LLC
Cover/Interior Designer: Page2, LLC
Senior Content Licensing Specialist: Keri Johnson
Manager, Digital Production: Janean A. Utley
Compositor: Page2, LLC
Printer: RR Donnelley

Cover photo: Carlos Caetano/Shutterstock.com

All credits appearing on page iv or at the end of the book are considered to be an extension of the copyright page.

The Internet addresses listed in the text were accurate at the time of publication. The inclusion of a website does not indicate an endorsement by the authors or McGraw-Hill, and McGraw-Hill does not guarantee the accuracy of the information presented at these sites.

www.mhhe.com

www.elt.mcgraw-hill.com

The **McGraw-Hill** Companies

A Special Thank You

The Interactions/Mosaic 6th edition team wishes to thank our extended team: teachers, students, administrators, and teacher trainers, all of whom contributed invaluably to the making of this edition.

Maiko Berger, **Ritsumeikan Asia Pacific University**, Oita, Japan • Aaron Martinson, **Sejong Cyber University**, Seoul, Korea • Aisha Osman, Egypt • Amy Stotts, **Chubu University**, Aichi, Japan • Charles Copeland, **Dankook University**, Yongin City, Korea • Christen Savage, **University of Houston**, Texas, USA • Daniel Fitzgerald, **Metropolitan Community College**, Kansas, USA • Deborah Bollinger, **Aoyama Gakuin University**, Tokyo, Japan • Duane Fitzhugh, **Northern Virginia Community College**, Virginia, USA • Gregory Strong, **Aoyama Gakuin University**, Tokyo, Japan • James Blackwell, **Ritsumeikan Asia Pacific University**, Oita, Japan • Janet Harclerode, **Santa Monica College**, California, USA • Jinyoung Hong, **Sogang University**, Seoul, Korea • Lakkana Chaisaklert, **Rajamangala University of Technology Krung Thep**, Bangkok, Thailand • Lee Wonhee, **Sogang University**, Seoul, Korea • Matthew Gross, **Konkuk University**, Seoul, Korea • Matthew Stivener, **Santa Monica College**, California, USA • Pawadee Srisang, **Burapha University**, Chantaburi, Thailand • Steven M. Rashba, **University of Bridgeport**, Connecticut, USA • Sudatip Prapunta, **Prince of Songkla University**, Trang, Thailand • Tony Carnerie, **University of California San Diego**, California, USA

Photo Credits

Page 2: Photo by Scott Dunn/Getty Images; 4 (left): Vicky Kasala/Getty Images, (right): Dave & Les Jacobs/Getty Images; 6 (top): Doug Sherman/Geofile, (bottom): Tetra Images/Getty Images; 9: Marili Forastieri/Getty Images; 15: © Fancy Collection/SuperStock; 20: Kraig Scarbinsky/Getty Images; 25: AFP/Getty Images; 28 (left): Purestock/SuperStock, (right): J. Hardy/PhotoAlto; 29 (top): Comstock Images/Jupiter Images, (bottom): © Picturenet/Blend Images LLC; 38: Thomas Northcut/Photodisc/Getty Images; 40 (top): J. Hardy/PhotoAlto, (bottom): Photodisc/Getty Images; 41: Comstock/Getty Images; 43: © Lars A. Niki; 44: Kathrin Ziegler/Getty Images; 47: commerceandculturestock/Getty Images; 48 (top to bottom): © The McGraw-Hill Companies, Inc./Laurence Waucampt, photographer, Aurora Open/SuperStock, © Royalty-Free/Corbis Images; 56: © Royalty-Free/Corbis; 58 (top to bottom): Comstock/Jupiter Images, © Ingram Publishing/Alamy, © Rubberball/Alamy, Comstock Images, Copyright © Foodcollection, Copyright © FoodCollection, Design Pics/Darren Greenwood, © PhotoAlto/PictureQuest; 60 (top): © Jose Luis Pelaez Inc/Blend Images LLC, (bottom): Photolink/Getty Images; 61 (top): © The McGraw-Hill Companies, (bottom): © Image Source; 65: Ingram Publishing; 71 (top left): Ingram Publishing, (top right): © Creatas/PunchStock, (middle left): Brand X Pictures, (middle center): JGI/Blend Images LLC, (middle right): Design Pics/Kristy-Anne Glubish, (bottom): Tetra Images/Getty Images; 76: Tom Merton/Getty Images; 80: © Jon Feingersh/Blend Images LLC; 81: Purestock/SuperStock; 83 (left): Fotosearch/Photolibrary, (right): Design Pics/Don Hammond; 87: PhotoAlto/Veer; 94: Will & Deni Mcintyre/Getty Images; 96: © Digital Vision/PunchStock; 99: © image100/Corbis; 104: Design Pics/Kristy-Anne Glubish; 112: KidStock/Getty Images; 114 (top to bottom): © USDA, Photo by Ken Hammond, Brand X Pictures/Punchstock, MIXA/Getty Images; 116: Jim Sugar/Corbis; 117: REUTERS/Corbis; 120 (left to right): Ingram Publishing, Charles O'Rear/Corbis; 127: Ingram Publishing; 130: Digital Vision/PunchStock; 134 (top): The Fat Kitchen by Steen, Jan Havicksz (1625/26-79), © John Lund/Drew Kelly/Blend Images LLC; 138: Westend61 GmbH/Alamy; 139 (top to bottom): Burke/Triolo Productions/Brand X Pictures/Getty Images, Product of Hotlix ® 2006 www.hotlix.com – Graphic design & photography www.yrigollen.com, Burke/Triolo Productions/Brand X Pictures/Getty Images; 145: Creatas/PunchStock; 148: Jacob Halaska/Getty Images; 150 (top left to right): © Comstock Images/Masterfile, Rubberball/Getty Images, © Masterfile; 150 (bottom): David Ashley/Corbis, David Ashley/Corbis; 153: National Science Foundation; 154 (top): Medioimages/Photodisc/Getty Images, (bottom): Aaron Roeth Photography; 155: Wolfgang Kaehler/Corbis; 158 (top left): Melba Photo Agency/PunchStock, (top right): Brand X Pictures/Jupiterimages, (bottom): Hisham Ibrahim/Getty Images; 162 (top): Royalty-Free/CORBIS, (bottom): Ingram Publishing; 163 (top): Tetra Images/Getty Images, (bottom): Design Pics/Deddeda; 168: Frans Lanting/Corbis; 170 (top left): Royalty-Free/CORBIS, (top right): Jules Frazier/Getty Images, (bottom left to right): Royalty-Free/Corbis, Author's Image/PunchStock; 173: C Squared Studios/Getty Images; 178: © Digital Vision/PunchStock; 179 (top left): Royalty-Free/CORBIS, (top right): © Stockbyte/PictureQuest, (bottom): © Elmer Frederick Fischer/Corbis

Text Credit

Page 79: "Most Popular College Majors for Women" by Jenna Goudreau, *Forbes*, 8.10.10. Copyright © 2010 Forbes, Inc. Used with permission.

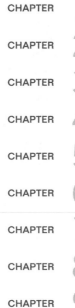

Table of Contents

A 21st-Century Course for the Modern Student

Interactions/Mosaic prepares students for university classes by fully integrating every aspect of student life. Based on 28 years of classroom-tested best practices, the new and revised content, fresh modern look, and new online component make this the perfect series for contemporary classrooms.

Proven Instruction that Ensures Academic Success

Modern Content:
From social networking to gender issues and from academic honesty to discussions of Skype, *Interactions/Mosaic* keeps students connected to learning by selecting topics that are interesting and relevant to modern students.

Emphasis on Vocabulary:
Each chapter teaches vocabulary intensively and comprehensively. This focus on learning new words is informed by more than 28 years of classroom testing and provides students with the exact language they need to communicate confidently and fluently.

NEW to *Interactions Access Reading* 6th Edition

- **3 Revised Chapters**, updated to reflect contemporary student life:
  Chapter 1: Neighborhoods, Cities, and Towns
  Chapter 3: Family and Friends
  Chapter 5: Men and Women
- **6 all-new readings** focusing on global topics and digital life
- **Over 80 new vocabulary words** that enhance proficiency
- **All new photos** showcase a modern, multicultural university experience

Practical Critical Thinking:

Students develop their ability to synthesize, analyze, and apply information from different sources in a variety of contexts: from comparing academic articles to negotiating informal conversations.

Digital Component:

The fully integrated online course offers a rich environment that expands students' learning and supports teachers' teaching with automatically graded practice, assessment, classroom presentation tools, online community, and more.

Highlights of *Interactions Access Reading* 6ᵗʰ Edition

Part 1: Reading Skills and Strategies
Each chapter begins with a text on an engaging, academic topic and teaches students the skills that they need to be successful.

Men and Women in Business

Before You Read

1 Interviewing Other Students Look at the chart below. Walk around the room and ask as many students as possible the three questions below. Write their answers in this chart. For Questions 1 and 2, use symbols to show the number of people who gave each answer. For example, ‖ = 2 people, ⫣ = 5 people. For Question 3, write your classmates' answers in words.

Question 1	Men's Answers		Women's Answers	
Is it important to have a high position at work?	Yes	No	Yes	No

Question 2	Men's Answers		Women's Answers	
When you have a problem at school or work, what do you like to do?	I usually solve it myself.	I usually ask for help.	I usually solve it myself.	I usually ask for help.

Question 3	Men's Answers		Women's Answers	
What does it mean when a person **nods** (moves the head up and down)?				

2 Critical Thinking: Understanding a Graph Look at the graph on page 79. Then discuss the following questions.

1. Which field has more women? About what percent (%) are women? About what percent are men?
2. Which field has more men? About what percent are men? Women?
3. Which field has an almost **equal** (same) number of women and men?
4. This graph is about college graduates in the United States in 2008. Do you think the numbers are different today? Are the numbers different in other countries?

Men and Women in Three Fields: Engineering, Education, and Business

3 Previewing Vocabulary Read the words in the list. They are words from the next reading. Listen to their pronunciation. Do not look them up in a dictionary. Check (✓) the words that you don't know.

Nouns
- body language
- equality
- eye contact
- fields
- genders
- hierarchy
- position
- suggestions

Verbs
- communicate
- connect
- nod

Adjectives
- comfortable
- equal
- funny
- similar

> **Strategy**
>
> **Understanding New Words in a Reading**
> You do not always need to use a dictionary to find the meaning of a new word. Sometimes the meaning is in the sentence before or after the word.
>
> **Example**
> Men and women also have different body language. They have different ways to communicate with their face and body.
>
> (*Body language* means different ways to communicate with the face and body.)
>
> Sometimes the meaning is after the phrase *in other words.*
>
> **Example**
> Experts are paying attention to the differences in the ways businesswomen and men think and communicate—in other words, talk with and understand other people.
>
> (*Communicate* means to talk with and understand other people.)

Communication for the Modern Student
A focus on real-life and academic communication based on engaging readings prepares students for success in school and in life.

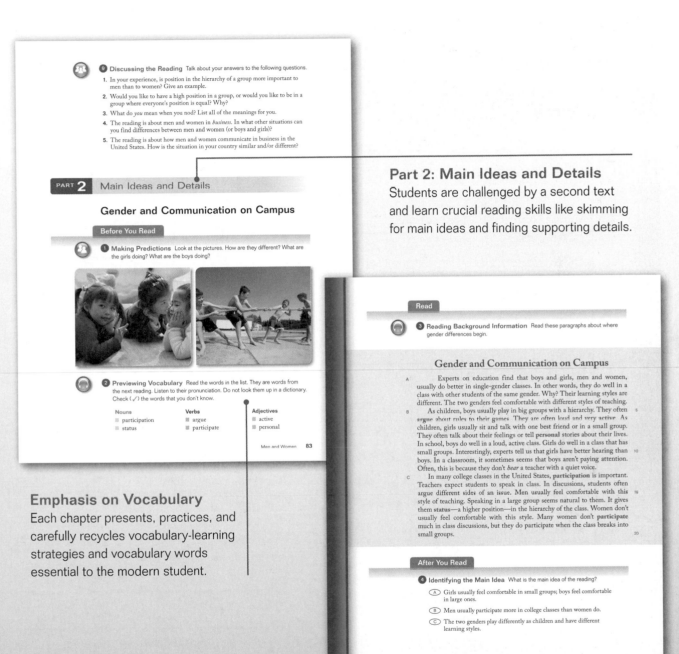

9 Discussing the Reading Talk about your answers to the following questions.

1. In your experience, is position in the hierarchy of a group more important to men than to women? Give an example.

2. Would you like to have a high position in a group, or would you like to be in a group where everyone's position is equal? Why?

3. What do *you* mean when you nod? List all of the meanings for you.

4. The reading is about men and women in *business*. In what other situations can you find differences between men and women (or boys and girls)?

5. The reading is about how men and women communicate in business in the United States. How is the situation in your country similar and/or different?

PART 2 Main Ideas and Details

Gender and Communication on Campus

Before You Read

1 Making Predictions Look at the pictures. How are they different? What are the girls doing? What are the boys doing?

2 Previewing Vocabulary Read the words in the list. They are words from the next reading. Listen to their pronunciation. Do not look them up in a dictionary. Check (✓) the words that you don't know.

Nouns	Verbs	Adjectives
☐ participation	☐ argue	☐ active
☐ status	☐ participate	☐ personal

Men and Women **83**

Part 2: Main Ideas and Details

Students are challenged by a second text and learn crucial reading skills like skimming for main ideas and finding supporting details.

Read

3 Reading Background Information Read these paragraphs about where gender differences begin.

Gender and Communication on Campus

A Experts on education find that boys and girls, men and women, usually do better in single-gender classes. In other words, they do well in a class with other students of the same gender. Why? Their learning styles are different. The two genders feel comfortable with different styles of teaching.

B As children, boys usually play in big groups with a hierarchy. They often argue about rules to their games. They are often loud and very active. As children, girls usually sit and talk with one best friend or in a small group. They often talk about their feelings or tell **personal** stories about their lives. In school, boys do well in a loud, active class. Girls do well in a class that has small groups. Interestingly, experts tell us that girls have better hearing than boys. In a classroom, it sometimes seems that boys aren't paying attention. Often, this is because they don't *hear* a teacher with a quiet voice.

C In many college classes in the United States, **participation** is important. Teachers expect students to speak in class. In discussions, students often argue different sides of an issue. Men usually feel comfortable with this style of teaching. Speaking in a large group seems natural to them. It gives them **status**—a higher position—in the hierarchy of the class. Women don't usually feel comfortable with this style. Many women don't **participate** much in class discussions, but they do participate when the class breaks into small groups.

After You Read

4 Identifying the Main Idea What is the main idea of the reading?

Ⓐ Girls usually feel comfortable in small groups; boys feel comfortable in large ones.

Ⓑ Men usually participate more in college classes than women do.

Ⓒ The two genders play differently as children and have different learning styles.

84 CHAPTER 5

Emphasis on Vocabulary

Each chapter presents, practices, and carefully recycles vocabulary-learning strategies and vocabulary words essential to the modern student.

Using Inclusive Language

FOCUS

Understanding Language and Sexism

Sexism is the belief that one gender (male or female) is better than the other gender. Many people believe that language can be *sexist*; that is, language can give us the idea that men are better or more important than women. Some common phrases in English traditionally name men first; for example, *men and women, husbands and wives,* and *Mr. and Mrs.*

There used to be words for jobs that included the idea of only men doing these jobs—words such as *fireman* and *mailman.* Some people believe these words give us the idea that only men can fight fires or deliver the mail. Therefore, most people now use the words *fire fighter* and *mail carrier* to include the idea of both men and women. To make language more *gender neutral* or equal, people are changing the way they use langauge.

① **Matching Words** Read the words below. Match the words in Column A with the gender-neutral words in Column B.

Column A (only male or female)

1. ___f___ man-made
2. _____ mankind
3. _____ policeman
4. _____ chairman
5. _____ actress
6. _____ wife or husband
7. _____ housewife
8. _____ salesman
9. _____ waiter/waitress
10. _____ stewardess
11. _____ headmaster
12. _____ manpower

Column B (either male or female)

a. chair or chairperson
b. salesperson
c. spouse
d. police officer
e. flight attendant
f. not natural, made by humans
g. server (in a restaurant)
h. humanity, people, human beings
i. actor
j. homemaker
k. staff, workers
l. principal, director

Part 3: Practical English

From how to navigate a college campus to reading blogs, students engage in topics that prepare them for success in the real world.

FOCUS

Using Gender-Neutral Possessive Adjectives

Possessive adjectives show gender; *his* is used But sometimes we don't know if a noun is male or both genders. In such cases, you can use *his or her* noun plural and use the possessive adjective *their,* include both.

Every student needs **his** laptop.

(*His* refers to a male. We can use this only when

Every student needs **his or her** laptop.

(Using *his or her* includes both male and fema

Students need **their** laptops.

(Making the sentence plural includes

3. The _____ _____and.
4. A doctor will pay a lot _____ _____ education.

5. Some police officer parked _____ car on the street in front of my house.
6. My teacher, Ms. Smith, always answers _____ e-mail from us.
7. Every teacher needs to know _____ subject well.

8. Mr. Jones is my Information Technology 101 professor, and I love _____ class.
9. Every person can make _____ own decision.

10. A man can change _____ mind, and a woman can change _____ mind, too.

Topics for the Modern Student

Engaging social and academic topics draw the student in, making learning more engaging and more efficient.

Part 4: Vocabulary Practice
The final section is dedicated to reviewing and intensively practicing words students learned throughout the chapter.

Results for Students A carefully structured program presents and practices academic skills and strategies purposefully, leading to strong student results and more independent learners.

Scope and Sequence

Critical-Thinking Skills	Vocabulary Building	Language Skills
Making predictions Synthesizing and discussing ideas from a reading	Previewing vocabulary Understanding new words with *is, are, is like*, and *are like* Developing vocabulary strategies Understanding prepositions	Understanding large numbers Using prepositions
Analyzing predictions from the past and about the future Identifying a good summary Synthesizing and discussing ideas from a reading Safely using passwords on websites	Previewing vocabulary Understanding new words from examples Understanding new words: using punctuation clues	Reviewing verb tenses
Using a graphic organizer to organize ideas in an essay Making predictions Using the Internet as a dictionary tool	Previewing vocabulary Understanding new words: using pictures Using a print dictionary: alphabetical order Understanding pronouns	Interviewing other students Using pronouns
Analyzing and comparing answers Finding important details Synthesizing and discussing ideas from a reading	Previewing vocabulary Finding meaning after *which* or *who* Identifying and matching vocabulary words and definitions Understanding pronouns Changing nouns to adjectives Identifying body parts Identifying opposites	Giving advice Understanding guide words in a dictionary Describing illnesses Understanding pronouns

Scope and Sequence

Chapter	Reading Selections	Reading Skills and Strategies
5 Men and Women **p76**	*Men and Women in Business* *Gender and Communication on Campus*	Prereading: Thinking about the topic Previewing vocabulary Understanding new words in a reading Understanding main ideas and details Identifying a good summary Making predictions Reading faster: reading in phrases
6 Sleep and Dreams **p94**	*The Purpose of Sleep and Dreams* *A Dream Narrative*	Prereading: Thinking about the topic Previewing vocabulary Finding the meaning of new words: meaning after *or* Identifying details Thinking about the topic Identifying the main idea
7 Work and Lifestyles **p112**	*Volunteering* *My Special Year*	Prereading: Thinking about the topic Previewing vocabulary Finding the meaning of new words: looking at colons Understanding sentences with the word *that* Finding the main ideas and important details Checking vocabulary
8 Food and Nutrition **p130**	*New Foods, New Diets* *Eating Bugs*	Prereading: Thinking about the topic Previewing a reading Previewing vocabulary Identifying the main ideas in a reading Using opposites to understand a new word Identifying the topic in a paragraph Finding details

Critical-Thinking Skills	Vocabulary Building	Language Skills
Understanding a graph Making predictions Recognizing and writing conclusions	Previewing vocabulary Checking vocabulary	Interviewing other students Discussing ideas from the reading Understanding language and sexism Using gender-neutral possessive adjectives
Understanding mood Finding the meaning of new words from context Searching for and analyzing information on the Internet	Previewing vocabulary Understanding words from their parts Finding the meaning of words: meaning after *or* Previewing vocabulary Understanding pronouns	Interviewing students Discussing ideas from the reading
Organizing details using a T-chart Making inferences Reading and analyzing a chart	Previewing vocabulary Understanding words from their parts: suffixes	Understanding sentences with the word *that*
Organizing details using a graphic organizer Reading and analyzing a chart Analyzing information	Previewing vocabulary Using opposites to understand a new word Figuring out words with more than one meaning	Interviewing other students

Scope and Sequence

Critical-Thinking Skills	Vocabulary Building	Language Skills
Reaching a conclusion: paying attention to evidence	Previewing vocabulary	Understanding words for directions
Synthesizing and discussing ideas from a reading	Understanding words for directions	Stating and explaining opinions
Reading a website and analyzing information	Understanding words from their prefixes	
Identifying support for opinions	Using *go* + verb + *-ing* for activities	
Understanding relationships between ideas	Previewing vocabulary	Interviewing other students
Using a graphic organizer to show relationships	Understanding words from their parts: *over* in a word	Using facts and figures
Making inferences	Understanding words that can be more than one part of speech	
Discussing and synthesizing a reading		
Reading and analyzing a graph		
Reading and analyzing a pie chart		
Comparing facts and figures		

CHAPTER 1

Neighborhoods, Cities, and Towns

College is the best
time of your life…

Author Unknown

In Part 1, you will read about the different types of services and activities that colleges offer their students. In the rest of this chapter, you will about read about, discuss, and explore the college experience: housing, academics, and social life.

Connecting to the Topic

1. What do you see in the photo? *+ next page*

2. Name five adjectives to describe this city.

3. Do you live in a big city or a small town? Describe where you live.

College Campuses Today

Before You Read

1 Thinking About the Topic. Discuss these questions with a partner.

1. Look at the pictures below. What do you see? What's happening?
2. How is this the same as your school? How is it different?

Strategy

Making a Prediction About the Topic

Before you read an article, it's good to have an idea in mind about the **topic** *def.*
(the subject of the article). Follow these steps before you begin to read:

• Look at the title.
• Look at the pictures and diagrams.

2 Making a Prediction Look at the title and photos for the reading on page 6.
Write the answers to the questions.

What is this reading about? What do the pictures in the reading show you?

Pronounce

Listen ?

3 Previewing Vocabulary Read the words in the list. They are words from the article. Listen to their pronunciation. Do not look them up in a dictionary. Check (✓) the words that you don't know.

Nouns
- apartment building
- art gallery
- campus/ campuses
- college/colleges
- computers
- dormitory/ dormitories (dorm/dorms)
- entertainment

- health center
- learning resources center
- population
- snack bars
- thousand
- transportation
- tutor
- university/ universities

Verbs
- exercise
- give/gives
- go
- happen/happens
- have/has
- help/helps
- take/takes

Adjectives
- modern
- several
- wonderful

Strategy

Understanding New Words: Look for *Is*, *Are*, *Is like*, and *Are like*

You do not always need to use a dictionary to find the meaning of a new word. Sometimes you can find the meaning of a new word after the word *is* or *are* in the sentence.

Example

Population **is** the number of people in a city or country.

(*Population* = the number of people in a city or country.)

Example

A campus **is** the land and buildings of a university.

(*Campus* = the land and buildings of a university.)

The words *is like* or *are like* help with the meaning of a word, too. *Like* can mean *def* "similar to" (= almost the same as).

A campus is like a small town.
Tutors are like teachers

4 Understanding New Words The meanings of these words are in the next article. Find the words and circle their meanings in the article.

| dormitory | learning resources center | shuttle | tutor |

Look over the **bold** words in the article for two more words that are new to you. Write them here.

_____   _____

⑤ Reading an Article Read the following article. Then do the activities.

[handwritten top margin: 3 parts ⟨ b — intro / m — body / end — con]

College Campuses Today

[handwritten: intro]

[handwritten left margin: Pronounce bold / Read \ Listen]

[handwritten left margin: ? Pop of town / ? " " city / ? Wch is bigger ?]

A A college is a **wonderful** place. It is like a town or small city in **several** ways. One way is **population**. In general, the population of a town is less than (<) 10,000 people. A city is more than (>) 10,000 people. In the United States, many **colleges** and **universities** have several **thousand** students. For example, Pasadena City College, in California, has almost 30,000 students. Miami-Dade College, in Florida, has 174,000 students on eight **campuses**! In other ways, too, a **modern** college is like a small city. *[5]*

Population in U.S. Colleges and Universities

	0	5,000,000	10,000,000	15,000,000	20,000,000	30,000,000
Fall 2000						
Fall 2012						

[handwritten left margin: ? Wht is a / snack / bar]

[handwritten left margin: ? When / would / stud. go to / a health / center on / campus]

[handwritten: body]

▲ Transportation on campus

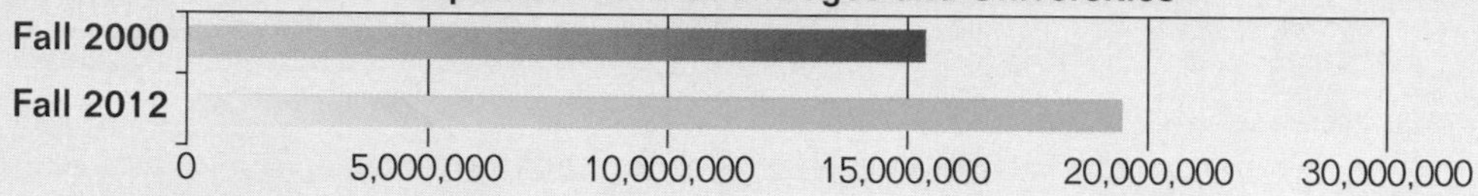

B Like a city, many colleges have everything for student life. There are **dormitories**, for example. (A dormitory is an **apartment building** for students.) There are places to eat: dining rooms, coffee shops, and **snack bars**. There is a student store, with food, clothes, and **computers**. There is a **health center**, with doctors and dentists. There is often a **shuttle** for students. (A shuttle is a bus. It takes students from one place on campus to another.) *[10] [15]*

[handwritten left margin: ? Wt kind / of entertain.]

C Like any city, a college campus has **entertainment**. There is often a radio station or theater. There is a sports center, where students **exercise**: they run, swim, or play games. They watch sports, too. There are music rooms, where students play piano, for example. There is a student **art gallery**. *[20]*

[handwritten left margin: ? ESL / ? 9.6 (p. 7)]

D Of course, students go to college for an education. But learning happens in many places, not only a classroom. One important place is the **learning resources center**. This is like a library, but it also has computers and **tutors**. (A tutor is a teacher who helps one student with questions or problems.) Another important place is the ESL (English as a Second Language) Center. Here, there is help with the English language. *[25]*

E As we see, a college is like a small city. It is a place to live. It has food, clothes, doctors, and **transportation**. It has entertainment. And, yes, it gives students an education, too. *[30]*

[handwritten: con]

▲ A student art gallery

6 **Identifying the Main Ideas** Complete the sentences. Choose the best answer for each blank.

1. "College Campuses Today" is about _____.

     Ⓐ the population of colleges and universities in the United States

     Ⓑ how a college campus is similar to a small city

     Ⓒ why a college education is important

2. On a college campus, there are places to _____.

     Ⓐ live and study

     Ⓑ have a good time

     Ⓒ both A and B

7 **Vocabulary Check** Write a word for each definition. Use words from the reading.

1. an apartment building for students = _dormitory_

2. a bus = _Shuttle_

3. similar to a library, with computers and tutors = _LRC_

4. a teacher for one student = _tutor_

8 **Making Good Guesses** Complete the sentence. Look at the reading and choose the best answer.

The writer of "College Campuses Today" probably thinks _____.

     Ⓐ there are too many students at some colleges

     Ⓑ a college campus is a good place

     Ⓒ students learn things only in classrooms

9 **Discussing Ideas from the Reading** Answer these questions with a partner.

Who is from a big city? small? town? Popul?

1. Is your city large or small?

2. What is the population of your city?

Who went to college or univ in your town?

3. What is the population of your school?

4. What kinds of restaurants are usually on campus?

5. What entertainment does your school or city have?

6. Look at the diagram on page 6. How is the population of college and university students changing in the US? Make one comment.

Understanding Large Numbers Look at the words for large numbers below. Read the words out loud with a partner.

[handwritten: Read together Geet in pairs. : Pronounce . do #11.]

150	one hundred fifty
200	two hundred
3,000	three thousand
4,500	four thousand five hundred
5,350	five thousand three hundred fifty
6,475	six thousand four hundred seventy-five
70,000	seventy thousand
80,950	eighty thousand nine hundred fifty
100,000	one hundred thousand
950,632	nine hundred fifty thousand six hundred thirty-two
1,000,000	one million
15,700,000	fifteen million seven hundred thousand
23,570,600	twenty-three million five hundred seventy thousand six hundred

[handwritten: Use for review]

 **Understanding Large Numbers: Information Gap**

Follow these directions:

Step 1: Work with a partner. One of you is Student A. One is Student B.

Step 2: Student A looks at page 191. Student B looks at page 192.

Student A

Ask your partner the questions below. Write your partner's answers in the chart on page 191.

Questions:

1. What is the population of Manhattan, New York?
2. What is the population of Arizona State University?
3. What is the population of Los Angeles, California?
4. What is the population of Orlando, Florida?
5. What is the population of Boston University?
6. What is the population of DePaul University?
7. What is the population of Washington, D.C.?

Student B

Ask your partner the questions on page 9. Write your partner's answers in the chart on page 192.

Questions:

1. What is the population of New York University?
2. What is the population of Tempe, Arizona?
3. What is the population of the University of Southern California?
4. What is the population of the University of Central Florida?
5. What is the population of Boston, Massachusetts?
6. What is the population of Chicago, Illinois?
7. What is the population of George Washington University?

PART 2   Main Ideas and Details

An Email from College

Before You Read

1 **Making Predictions** Look at the picture. Where are these students? What are they doing?

Prounounce .

2 **Previewing Vocabulary** Read the words in the list. They are words from the next reading. Listen to their pronunciation. Do not look them up in the dictionary. Check (✓) the words that you don't know.

Nouns	Verb	Prepositions
▪ conversation	▪ practice	▪ across from
▪ cooking		▪ in
▪ email		▪ on (a street)
▪ neighborhood		▪ on campus
		▪ on the corner (of…)

3 **Reading an Email** Read the following email. Then do the activities.

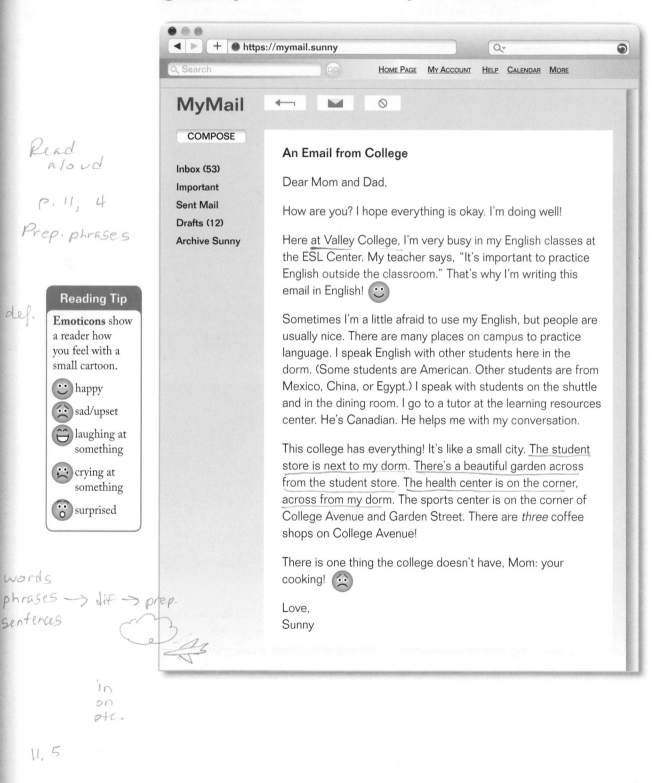

https://mymail.sunny

HOME PAGE   MY ACCOUNT   HELP   CALENDAR   MORE

MyMail

COMPOSE

Inbox (53)
Important
Sent Mail
Drafts (12)
Archive Sunny

Reading Tip

Emoticons show a reader how you feel with a small cartoon.

happy

sad/upset

laughing at something

crying at something

surprised

An Email from College

Dear Mom and Dad,

How are you? I hope everything is okay. I'm doing well!

Here at Valley College, I'm very busy in my English classes at the ESL Center. My teacher says, "It's important to practice English outside the classroom." That's why I'm writing this email in English! :)

Sometimes I'm a little afraid to use my English, but people are usually nice. There are many places on campus to practice language. I speak English with other students here in the dorm. (Some students are American. Other students are from Mexico, China, or Egypt.) I speak with students on the shuttle and in the dining room. I go to a tutor at the learning resources center. He's Canadian. He helps me with my conversation.

This college has everything! It's like a small city. The student store is next to my dorm. There's a beautiful garden across from the student store. The health center is on the corner, across from my dorm. The sports center is on the corner of College Avenue and Garden Street. There are *three* coffee shops on College Avenue!

There is one thing the college doesn't have, Mom: your cooking! :(

Love,
Sunny

4 **Identifying the Main Topic** What is the main topic of the email? Choose one answer.

- (A) places where Sunny practices English
- (B) Sunny's college neighborhood
- (C) Sunny's life at college

5 **Finding Details** Read Sunny's story again. Then look at the map of her college. Answer the question below the map.

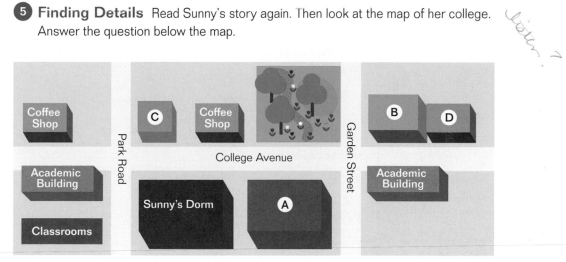

▲ Map of one part of a college campus

Where are these places? Write the letters from the map on the lines.

1. the student store _A_

2. a coffee shop _D_

3. the sports center _B_

4. the health center _C_

Culture Note

In the United States, community colleges (two-year colleges) don't usually have dormitories (dorms). Students live at home or in apartments. Four-year colleges and universities have dormitories. Some students live there, some live at home, and some live in an apartment with other students. In your home country, are there dorms on campuses?

Strategy

Following Directions in Textbooks

Read the following directions and look at the examples. You will find directions like these in your textbook activities.

Read (handwritten note)

Directions	Examples
1. Circle the word.	(building)
2. Copy the word: street.	street
3. Underline the word.	building
4. Circle the letter of the correct answer.	Which word is a country? a. summer (b.) Mexico c. park
5. Fill in the blank.	My name ___is___ Sunny.
6. Write your name on the line.	___Sunny Kim___
7. Correct the mistake.	She's from Korea.
8. Choose the best answer.	Which word means "dormitory"? (A) dorm (B) apartment (C) house

(handwritten margin notes: "?" "," "?" ".")

6 **Following Textbook Directions** Now follow these textbook directions.

(handwritten margin note: In groups of 3: 6, 7, 8, 9)

1. Circle the name of a city.

   Brazil   Indonesia   Paris   Egypt   Alaska

2. Find the name of a person below and copy it on the line.

   Mexico _____   California _____

   the USA _____   Sunny ___Sunny___

3. Underline the words for buildings.

   I'm at my dorm now, but I'm going to the cafeteria in ten minutes.

4. Circle the letter of a place near Sunny's dormitory.

   a. snack bar   **b.** art gallery   **c.** health center   **d.** ESL center

5. Write the name of your country on the line. ⌣ _____

6. Correct the mistakes.

Egypt
I live in ~~egipt~~.

7. Choose the name of a country.

(A) American (B) Japan (C) Mexican (D) Egyptian

7 **Building Vocabulary** Write the words from the box in the correct places on the chart. *Check after*

American	dorm	learning resource center
art gallery	Egypt	Mexico
Canadian	English	music practice rooms
China	ESL center	sports center
classroom	garden	
coffee shop	health center	

Countries	Places on campus	Words that mean "From or of a place"

8 Completing Sentences Fill in each blank with a word from the box. (Use one word three times.) on

across	in	next	on

1. My family's house is _____on_____ the main street of our small town.
2. But here, at Valley College, I live _____in_____ a dorm.
3. There are several small coffee shops here. There's one _____across_____ from my dorm.
4. There's a very good coffee shop _____on_____ the corner of Park Road and College Avenue.
5. There's a wonderful coffee shop _____next_____ to the ESL Center.
6. I'm happy to live _____on_____ campus. I love coffee!

9 Discussing the Reading Discuss these questions with a group. Then share your answers with the class.

1. What buildings are on your campus or near your school? Where are they?
2. Are there people from different countries at your school or in your neighborhood? What countries are they from?
3. Draw a map of your neighborhood, campus, or one part of your school. Describe the map to the other members of your group.

DO HW **10 Writing in Your Journal** Choose one topic below. Write about it for five minutes. Use five vocabulary words that you have learned in this chapter.

- your neighborhood (Describe it.)
- big cities (Do you like them? Why or why not?)
- places where you practice English
- your college/university/school

PART 3 Practical English

Read

1 Advice About College All students want to do well in college or university. What are some the ways to help you do well? Read the article.

Keys to Success in College

▲ Dr. Laura Phillips,
educational consultant

Educational consultant Dr. Laura Phillips is an expert on how college students learn. Parents pay her hundreds of dollars to give their children advice about how to do well in college. Here are four of Dr. Phillips' tips for success in college.

1. Talk to your professor

Professors have special "office hours," which are times when students can come and talk to them. Many students never use this great opportunity. You usually have to make an appointment. You can ask your professor questions, ask for advice about ideas for papers, or even ask about a test. Talking to your professors tells the professor that you are serious and interested.

2. Use study groups

Students in most U.S. college classes form study groups, which are groups of several students who meet outside class to help each other. If you are a foreign student, this is even more important. Students discuss the class in native English, which will give you ideas for language you can use in papers or on tests.

3. Study in small blocks of time

Don't try to study everything the night before a test. Experts find that you learn much better if you break your study time into small "blocks" or pieces. For example, study one hour three times a day. Do this for three days. You will remember more than if you study one day for nine hours.

4. Learn to budget your time. (Learn to use your time well.)

Get a good appointment book, which is like a calendar with hours and days of the week. Smart phones also have calendar applications. Write down your assignments (the work you have to do) and the hours you have available each day to work on those assignments. Don't leave work until the last day.

2 **Using Your Vocabulary Strategies** Complete the definitions of these words.

1. An educational consultant is _____.

2. Office hours are _____.

3. Study groups are _____.

4. An appointment book is _____.

3 Discussing the Reading Discuss these questions with a group. Share your three best study ideas with your group. Then share your ideas with the class.

1. How do you study for a test?
2. Do you write papers at the last moment? Why or why not?
3. What was your worst day in school? What was your best day?

HW

1 Reviewing Vocabulary Answer the questions below to show you understand these words.

1. Who lives in <u>dormitories</u>? _____ *students* _____.
2. What is something a <u>tutor</u> might help you with? _____
3. Name one thing you <u>discussed</u> today. _____
4. What is your favorite kind of <u>entertainment</u>? _____
5. Guess the <u>population</u> of New York City. _____
6. What is something a <u>shuttle</u> driver drives? _____
7. Name a <u>snack</u>. _____
8. Name three things you can see in an <u>art gallery</u>. _____

Rev.

2 Using Prepositions These are sentences from the chapter. Fill in the correct prepositions.

1. Students go to college ___for___ an education.
2. A shuttle takes students ___from___ one place on campus to another.
3. You can ask your professor ___for___ advice.
4. Learning happens ___in___ many places.
5. Students discuss the class ___in___ native English.
6. Tutors can help you ___with___ the subject.
7. Some students live ___at___ home.
8. Miami-Dade College, ___in___ Florida, has 174,000 students ___on___ eight campuses.

3 **Focusing on High-Frequency Words** Fill in the blanks with the best words from the box.

college	course	helps	place	questions
computers	help	like	places	teacher

Of _____course_____ (1), students go to _____college_____ (2) for an education. But learning happens in many _____places_____ (3), not only a classroom. One important _____place_____ (4) is the learning resources center. This is _____like_____ (5) a library, but it also has _____computers_____ (6) and tutors. (A tutor is a _____teacher_____ (7) who _____helps_____ (8) one student with _____questions_____ (9) or problems.) Another important place is the ESL (English as a Second Language) Center. Here, there is _____help_____ (10) with the English language.

4 **Using New Words** Some adjectives do not work with some nouns. Look at the chart below. Put a check (✓) in the box if you can use the adjective with the noun. Put a question mark (?) if you're not sure. Put an (X) if you can't use the adjective with the noun.

Nouns	Adjectives					
	building	man	snack	computer	campus	photo
modern	✓	✓	X	✓	✓	?
beautiful	✓	X	X	X	✓	✓
busy	✓	✓	X	✓	✓	X
large	✓	✓	✓	✓	✓	✓
wonderful	✓	✓	✓	✓	✓	✓
serious	X	✓	X	X	X	X
interested	X	✓	X	X	X	X

Building Vocabulary Complete the crossword puzzle with words from the box. These words are from Chapter 1.

budget	exercise	population	transportation
consultant	expert	shuttle	tutor
conversation	gallery	snack	wonderful
dorm	modern	tips	

Across

3. talk (n.)

10. how many people (n.)

11. make your body work (v.)

14. where you can see art (n.)

15. cars, buses, trains (n.)

Down

1. a little bit to eat (n.)

2. students sleep here (n.)

4. a bus or a van (n.)

5. very good (adj.)

6. person who gives advice (n.)

7. use time well (v.)

8. not old-fashioned (adj.)

9. good ideas (n.)

12. person who knows a lot (n.)

13. person who helps you learn (n.)

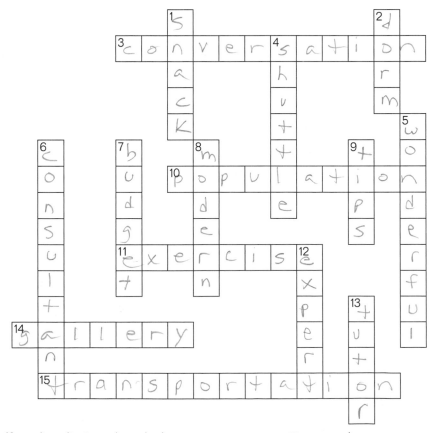

Key: *adj.* = adjective; *adv.* = adverb; *n.* = noun; *prep.* = preposition; *v.* = verb

Self-Assessment Log

Read the lists below. Check (✓) the strategies and vocabulary that you learned in this chapter. Look through the chapter or ask your instructor about the strategies and words that you do not understand.

Reading and Vocabulary-Building Strategies

☐ Making a prediction about the topic
☐ Understanding new words using *is* and *are*
☐ Understanding large numbers
☐ Following directions in textbooks
☐ Focusing on high-frequency words

Target Vocabulary

af.   *parts of speech*

Nouns

☐ apartment building
☐ art gallery
☐ campus/campuses
☐ college/colleges
☐ computers
☐ conversation
☐ cooking*
☐ dormitory/dormitories
☐ email
☐ entertainment
☐ health center
☐ learning resources center
☐ neighborhood
☐ population
☐ thousand*
☐ snack bars
☐ transportation
☐ tutor
☐ university/universities

Verbs

☐ exercise*
☐ give/gives*
☐ go*
☐ happen/happens*
☐ have/has*
☐ help/helps*
☐ practice*
☐ take/takes*

Adjectives

☐ modern*
☐ several*
☐ wonderful

Prepositions   *next to*

☐ across from*
☐ in*
☐ on* (a street)
☐ on campus
☐ on the corner (of…)

* These words are among the 1,000 most frequently used words in English.

2 Shopping and e-Commerce

"The safe way to double your money is to fold it over once and put it in your pocket."

Frank McKinney Hubbard
American writer and humorist

In this CHAPTER

In Part 1, you will read about online shopping and the first website to sell online. In the rest of this chapter, you will read about, explore, and discuss shopping, e-commerce, and how to create safe usernames and passwords.

Connecting to the Topic

1. What is the man in the photo shopping for? Discuss what he might be thinking about.

2. What do you like to shop for?

3. Where do you usually shop?

Internet Shopping

Before You Read

1 Thinking About the Topic   Ask different classmates the questions below. Write their answers in this chart. For students who answer yes to a question, ask them the second question in the box.

Question	Yes	No
1. Do you have a computer? How often do you use it?		
2. Do you use the Internet? What do you use it for?		
3. Did you know about the Internet ten years ago? When did you start using the Internet?		
4. Do you shop on the Internet? What do you buy on the Internet?		

FOCUS

Reviewing Verb Tenses

Regular verbs (such as *shop, start,* or *use*) end in *-ed* in the past tense, but many common verbs (such as *know*) are irregular in the past tense (do *not* end in *-ed*). You will work with irregular verbs on the next page.

live
move
work

Tense	Time	Subject	Verb Phrase
Past	Five years ago,	I you he/she/it we you they	**used** the Internet.
Present	Today,	I you	**use** the Internet.
		he/she/it	**uses** the Internet.
		we you they	**use** the Internet.

Tense	Time	Subject	Verb Phrase
Future	Soon,	I	**am going to use** the Internet.
		you	**will use** the Internet.
		he/she/it	**is going to use** it.
			will use it.
		we	**are going to use** it.
		you	**will use** it.

(is planning to)
(has the intention to)

be going to + Verb
will + verb

2 **Reviewing the Irregular Past Tense** Read the verbs in the chart below. Fill in the past tense of each verb. (Check a dictionary for verbs that you don't know.) With a partner, on a separate piece of paper, write one sentence with each past tense verb.

on board

Verb	Irregular Past Tense
be	*was, were*
begin	
buy	
drive	
have	
know	
quit	
sell	
think	

FYI Note

FYI Note

In natural spoken English, the pronunciation of *going to* is usually *gonna*.

3 **Reviewing the Future Tense** Now write one future sentence with each verb from the chart above. Use *be going to*.

4 **Previewing Vocabulary** Read the words and phrases below. Listen to their pronunciation. Do not look them up in a dictionary. Put a check mark (✓) next to the words that you don't know.

Repeat

Nouns
- categories (category)
- customers
- garage
- home improvement products
- information
- mall
- money
- prediction
- products
- profit
- scientists
- site
- stores
- percent
- virtual shopping mall

Verbs
- drove (drive)
- predict
- quit
- search
- sell

Adjectives
- gourmet
- huge
- online

Understanding New Words: Using Punctuation Clues
You do not always need to use a dictionary to find the meaning of a new word in a reading. Sometimes you can find the meaning of a new word in parentheses ( ) or after a dash —.

Examples
They sell products in many **categories** (groups of similar things).
   (*categories* = groups of similar things)

People can **search for**—look for—a book on the Internet.
   (*search for* = look for)

⑤ Understanding New Words: Using Punctuation Clues The meanings of these words are in the next article. Find the words and circle their meanings.

customers	online
gourmet	virtual shopping mall
home improvement products	

Read

⑥ Reading an Article Read the following article. Don't use your dictionary. If you don't know some words, try to figure out their meaning. Then do the activities.

Internet Shopping

A   Twenty-five years ago, very few people used the Internet. Only **scientists** and people in the government knew about the Internet and how to use it. This is changing very fast. Now almost everyone knows about the Internet, and many people are **online** (on the Internet) every day. When people think about the Internet, they often think about **information**. But now, more and   5
more, when people think about the Internet, they think about shopping.

B   Amazon.com was one of the first companies to try to **sell products** on the Internet. Jeff Bezos started the company. One day he made a **prediction** about the future. He saw that the World Wide Web was growing 2,000 **percent** a year. He predicted that it was going to continue to grow, and he   10
thought that shopping was going to move to the Internet. People were going to shop online. He **quit** his good job and **drove** across the country to Seattle,

▲ Amazon.com web page

Washington. There he started an online bookstore called Amazon.com. Bezos had very little **money**. The company began in a **garage**, and at first there were very few **customers** (people who buy things). 15

C   At the Amazon.com **site**, people can **search** for a book about a subject, find many different books about that subject, read what other people think about the books, order them by credit card, and get them in the mail in two days. This kind of bookstore was a new idea, but the business grew. In a few years, Amazon.com had 10 million customers and 20 25 30

sold 18 million different items in **categories** including books, CDs, toys, electronics, videos, DVDs, **home improvement products** (things that you use to fix up a house), software, and video games. Today, at a "**virtual shopping mall**"—a group of online **stores**—you can buy anything from **gourmet** food—special, usually expensive, food—to vacations. 35

D   Fifteen years ago, many people said, "Online shopping is crazy. Nobody can make money in an online company." They were wrong. Today, Jeff Bezos is a billionaire. More and more people are shopping online, and online companies are making a **profit**. It is a **huge** business. But some people **predict**, "Online business isn't going to grow anymore." They say, "customers are afraid of online crime, and they will stop shopping on the Internet." Are these people right? Nobody knows, but we'll soon find out. 40 45 50

▲ Jeff Bezos giving a speech about Amazon's new products

Class

7 Identifying the Main Ideas Complete the sentences. Choose the best answer.

1. The title of the article is "Internet Shopping." Another possible title is _____.

   Ⓐ "Internet Games"

   Ⓑ "Shopping on the Internet"

   Ⓒ "Information and the Internet"

2. The main idea of Paragraph A is _____.

   Ⓐ now more and more people use the Internet

   Ⓑ twenty-five years ago, very few people used the Internet

   Ⓒ scientists were first to use the Internet

3. The main idea of Paragraph B is _____.

   Ⓐ the Web was growing 2,000 percent a year

   Ⓑ Bezos started Amazon.com to sell products on the Internet

   Ⓒ Jeff Bezos quit his good job and moved to Seattle, Washington

4. The main idea of Paragraph C is _____.

   Ⓐ people can order books by credit card

   Ⓑ People can buy books and many other products from Amazon.com.

   Ⓒ people can search for a book on Amazon.com

5. Paragraph D is about _____.

   Ⓐ online shopping today and in the future

   Ⓑ Jeff Bezos

   Ⓒ people's fears about online shopping

8 Building Vocabulary Write a word for each definition. Use words from the reading.

1. on the Internet = online (#A)

2. people who buy things = customers

3. things that you use to fix up a house = hm imprvmt prods

4. a group of online stores = virtual shopping mall

5. special, usually expensive, food = gourmet food

9 Making Good Guesses Read the sentences. Choose the best answer.

1. We bought the house for $100,000. We sold it for $110,000. We made a $10,000 profit.

   A profit is probably _____.

   Ⓐ money that you lose in business

   Ⓑ money that you make in business

   Ⓒ money that you pay for a house

2. Jeff Bezos had very little money. The company began in a garage, and at first there were very few customers.

   A garage is probably a _____.
   - (A) big, expensive house
   - (B) place to play baseball
   - (C) small, inexpensive building for cars

Ask: Juan, what are going to do this weekend?

On board:
"I'm going to the movies."
↓
Juan said, "I'm..."
How do you know what Juan said?

F⊙CUS

Understanding Quotation Marks

Use quotation marks (" ") to tell exactly what someone says.

Example Jonathon said, "Our online business is growing every year."

10 Understanding Quotation Marks Look at Paragraph D in the article "Internet Shopping". What do some people predict? What do they say? Look for sentences in quotation marks. Copy the quotes here.

"Online shopping is crazy. Nobody can make $ in an online co."

prediction → "Online bsns isn't going to grow anymr."

"customers r afraid of online crime..."

11 Discussing the Reading Discuss the following questions. Then share your answers with the class.

1. Do you or your friends spend a lot of time online? Is this good or bad?
2. Do you think Internet shopping will become more or less popular in the next 10 years? Why?

PART 2 · Main Ideas and Details

Predicting the Future of Shopping

Before You Read

1 Thinking Ahead Look at the photos on page 28. Answer these questions.

1. What do you think the online shopper is buying?
2. What do you think the teenagers are doing at the mall?
3. In your opinion, which photo shows the future of shopping? Why?

▲ Shopping online: from home, work... from anywhere!

▲ Shopping at a mall

2 Previewing Vocabulary Read the words below. Listen to their pronunciation. Do not look them up in the dictionary. Put a check mark (✓) next to the words that you don't know.

Repeat

Nouns	Verbs	Adjectives	Adverb
◼ bags	◼ carry	◼ easy	◼ alone
◼ computers	◼ choose	◼ second	
◼ entertainment	◼ put		
◼ eye scan	◼ socialize		
◼ gym			
◼ purchases			

Strategy

Understanding New Words from Examples
Sometimes you can guess the meaning of a new word from examples. Often, these examples follow the words *such as*. → *introduces examples*
· examples help u understand the meaning of words

Example
Martha made many small purchases, **such as** books, CDs, and a couple of pens.
Amazon sells products in many categories, such as toys, gourmet food, and books.
You can buy anything at a virtual shopping mall, such as Amazon.com

? ex's of categories

? an ex of a VSM

3 Understanding New Words from Examples The meaning of each of these words is in the next article. Find the words and circle their meanings.

entertainment	purchases	socialize

4 **Reading an Article** Read the following article. Then do the activities.

Predicting the Future of Shopping

Main idea

A   There are different ideas about shopping in the future. Some people say, "Everybody is going to shop online, from home. There won't be any more real stores or shopping malls." But other people have a different picture of the future. They say, "There will still be shopping malls. In the future, many people will work at home, **alone**, on their **computers**. They'll want to go out to stores for their shopping. They'll want to **socialize**—be with other people." Maybe they're right.   5

B   But the stores of the future will probably be different from stores today.   10 Shopping in stores will be **easy**. First, people won't need to **carry** many **bags** from store to store. In stores, they will only choose products.   15 They won't carry them home. The stores will deliver most of their **purchases**, such as clothes and books, to their houses. **Second**, people   20

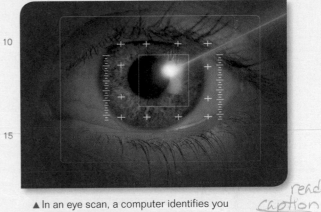

▲ In an eye scan, a computer identifies you from your eyes.

read caption

won't need to carry money or credit cards with them. An **eye scan** will identify their eyes and **put** their purchase on their credit card.

▲ The future shopping mall—where you can shop *and* go to the gym

C   Shopping malls will probably also be different from today. They won't only have big department stores   25 and many small stores. Malls will still be places for shopping and for **entertainment** such as movies. But in malls of the future, busy people will also do other things. They will   30 go to the doctor, the dentist, and the post office. They will go to the **gym**, too. Everybody agrees about one thing: shopping will be different in the future.   35

Strategy

Identifying the Topic and Main Idea of a Paragraph

A paragraph is about one main *topic* (subject). The topic is a *noun* or a *noun phrase* (one or more words about a person, place, or thing). A paragraph has one *main idea*—a sentence about the topic. The main idea is often the first sentence. For example, the *Internet* might be the topic of a paragraph, and the main idea might be: *The Internet is a great way to shop.*

⑤ **Identifying the Topic and Main Idea** Read the topics below. Write the letter of the paragraph from the reading (A, B, or C) next to each topic. Next, find the main idea of each paragraph. <u>Underline</u> the main idea in each paragraph in the reading.

_____B_____ shopping in stores

_____C_____ malls in the future

_____A_____ ideas about shopping in the future

Strategy

Summarizing

A *summary* has the main information of a paragraph or an article. It also has important details, but it doesn't have small details. Look at these two summaries of "Internet Shopping" from Part 1. Answer these questions: *Which summary is good? Why?*

A. Twenty-five years ago, most people didn't know about the Internet. Only scientists and the government used it. Today almost everyone finds information and shops online. Jeff Bezos began Amazon.com in a garage. The business grew fast. Soon it had 10 million customers and sold 18 million different items. At this online store, people can buy books, CDs, toys, electronics, gourmet food, and almost anything.

B. Many people are now shopping on the Internet. One example is the online store Amazon.com. Jeff Bezos began this site with books, but now it sells many different products. Amazon.com has a lot of customers, and it is making money.

Answer: The second summary is good. It has the main idea and important details. It doesn't have small details. The first summary is not good. It has small details.

6 **Identifying a Good Summary** Which is a good summary of the article "Predicting the Future of Shopping"? Why is it good? Why is the other not good?

A.   In the future, shopping will be different. It will be easy to shop in stores. People won't need to carry bags, money, or credit cards. In shopping malls, people will shop, find entertainment, and do practical things.

B.   In the future, people will work alone at home. They will want to go out and shop in stores. They will want to be with other people. Stores will be places to choose products. There will be eye scans in stores. Shopping malls are going to have stores, movies, doctors, dentists, post offices, and gyms.

No main idea
Unnec. details

7 **Thinking Critically** Predicting the future is a very difficult thing to do. Most people have a hard time doing this. Below are famous predictions from the past. What was wrong with each one? Discuss them with a group.

1. "I think there is a world market for maybe five computers."
   —A computer company executive, 1943

2. "No one is going to want a computer in their home."
   —A president of a large computer company, 1977

3. "Airplanes are interesting toys, but they have no military value."
   —A French professor of war, 1910

4. "Man will never reach the moon."
   —A scientist, 1952

5. "For most people, smoking is good for their health."
   —A doctor, quoted in a national magazine, 1963

Vocab. ?
what was wrong w/the prediction?
Board

8 **Discussing the Future** Below are some predictions about the next 50 years. Do you agree with them? On each line, write *likely* (will probably happen), *possible* (might happen), or *not likely* (probably won't happen). Then discuss your answers with a small group.

1. Every family will have a robot—a smart machine—to clean their house.

   _____

2. Scientists are going to have a cure for cancer in ten years. _____

3. Everyone in the world is going to use the Internet every day. _____

4. A very bad disease is going to kill 50 percent of all human beings.

   _____

5. No one is going to read books or magazines. They are going to listen to them on

   digital equipment such as computers and mp3 players. _____

6. No one in the world is going to smoke cigarettes. _____

7. Religion is going to become more important for people. _____

8. Everyone in the world is going to be able to speak English. _____

9. China is going to be the richest country in the world. _____

9 Writing in Your Journal Choose one topic below. Write about it for five minutes. Use some of the vocabulary that you have learned in this chapter.

- online shopping
- shopping malls
- your prediction about shopping in the future

? where do you see them ?

Passwords on Websites

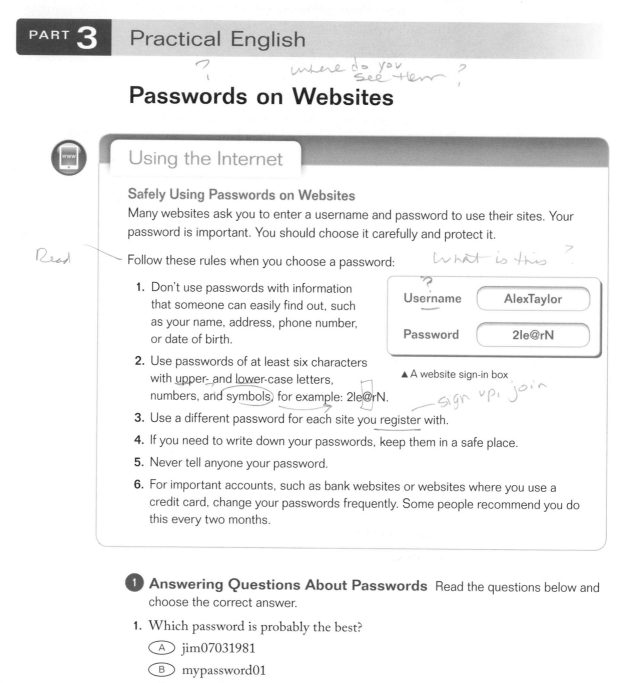

Using the Internet

Safely Using Passwords on Websites

Many websites ask you to enter a username and password to use their sites. Your password is important. You should choose it carefully and protect it.

Read

Follow these rules when you choose a password:

What is this ?

1. Don't use passwords with information that someone can easily find out, such as your name, address, phone number, or date of birth.

   | Username | AlexTaylor |
   | Password | 2le@rN |

2. Use passwords of at least six characters with upper- and lower-case letters, numbers, and symbols, for example: 2le@rN.

   ▲ A website sign-in box

   sign up, join

3. Use a different password for each site you register with.

4. If you need to write down your passwords, keep them in a safe place.

5. Never tell anyone your password.

6. For important accounts, such as bank websites or websites where you use a credit card, change your passwords frequently. Some people recommend you do this every two months.

1 Answering Questions About Passwords Read the questions below and choose the correct answer.

1. Which password is probably the best?

   (A) jim07031981

   (B) mypassword01

   (C) &YeS$66

2. When you register with a website, you usually _____.

- (A) pay money
- (B) fill out a form
- (C) change your password

3. When you think of a password, it's a good idea to _____.

- (A) use your last name to help you remember
- (B) use both symbols (such as $ and #) and letters
- (C) use your birth date

2 **Creating a Password** Write a new username and password below. Do not use your birth date, address, or name for the password. At the end of the week, see if you can remember it. (Because it's now written in your book, don't use this password on a website.) Write your name or your nickname in the username box.

Username	
Password	

▲ What's an example of a safe password?

1 **Answering True or False** Read the sentences below. Check (✓) True or False. New words from this chapter are underlined.

	True	False
1. You put a car in a garage.	☐	☐
2. When you make a profit, you have lost money.	☐	☐
3. When you are online, you are using the Internet.	☐	☐
4. You can drive or walk to a mall.	☐	☐
5. You can drive or walk to a virtual shopping mall.	☐	☐
6. Some people make predictions about the past.	☐	☐
7. When people work at home, they often work alone.	☐	☐

2 Listening: Fill in the Missing Words
Listen and fill in the words. Some of the words are new and some of the words are not new. Then check your work on page 24.

Twenty-five years _ago_ [1], very few people used the _Internet_ [2]. Only scientists and people in the government _knew_ [3] about the Internet and how to use it. This is changing very fast. Now almost everyone _knows_ [4] about the Internet, and many people are _online_ [5] (on the Internet) every day. When people _think_ [6] about the Internet, they often think about _information_ [7]. But now, more and more, when people think _about_ [8] the Internet, they think about shopping.

3 Using New Words
Write the correct word from the box in the sentences.

categories	online	profit	socialize
information	predict	scientists	summary

1. We sell products in many _categories_: electronics, sports equipment, and home improvement products.
2. _Scientists_ are trying to find a cure for cancer.
3. He never goes to the mall—he does all his shopping _online_.
4. I go to parties and see friends a lot because I like to _socialize_.
5. People often try to _predict_ the future, but they are often wrong.
6. When you study for a test, it helps to write a short _summary_ of what you read.
7. I use the Internet when I need _information_ about something.
8. He sold the company and made a huge _profit_—twenty million dollars.

4 **Focusing on High-Frequency Words** Read the paragraph below and fill in each blank with a word from the box. Then check your answers on page 29.

carry	easy	money	second
choose	eye	put	stores

Stores of the future will probably be different from _____stores_____ ₁ today. Shopping in stores will be _____ ₂. First, people won't need to __carry__ ₃ many bags from store to store. In stores, they will only __choose__ ₄ products. They won't carry them home. The stores will deliver most of their purchases, such as clothes and books, to their houses. __Second__ ₅, people won't need to carry __money__ ₆ or credit cards with them. An __eye__ ₇ scan will identify their eyes and __put__ ₈ their purchase on their credit card.

5 **Building Vocabulary** Complete the crossword puzzle on the next page with words from the box. These words are from Chapter 2. (Hint: Look for the easy answers first and fill in those words. This will help you with the more difficult words.)

Across

1. very big (adj.)
3. something you sell (n.)
5. money you can keep (n.)
6. to stop doing something (v.)
8. a place that sells books (n.)
10. groups of things (n.)
11. tell about the future (v.)
13. people who buy things (n.)
15. something you need to know (n.)
16. look for (v.)

Down

2. a place to park your car (n.)
4. something you do with your brain; (some people do this more than other people) (v.)
7. a word for food: It means "special, very good" (adj.)
9. people who work in science—biologists, physicists, geologists, medical researchers (n.)
11. a word that means this symbol: % (n.)
12. used a car (past tense) (v.)
14. a place on the Internet (n.)

bookstore
categories
customers
drove
garage

gourmet
huge
information
percent
predict

product
profit
quit
scientists
search

site
think

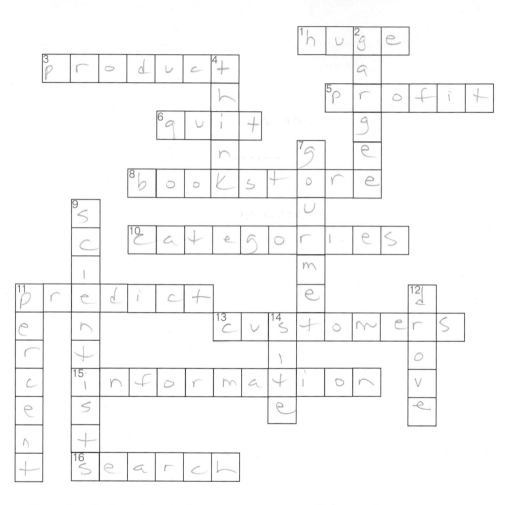

Across
1. huge
3. product
5. profit
6. quit
8. bookstore
10. categories
11. predict
13. customers
15. information
16. search

Key: *adj.* = adjective; *adv.* = adverb; *n.* = noun; *prep.* = preposition; *v.* = verb

Self-Assessment Log

Read the lists below. Check (✓) the strategies and vocabulary that you learned in this chapter. Look through the chapter or ask your instructor about the strategies and words that you do not understand.

Reading and Vocabulary-Building Strategies

☐ Reviewing verb tenses
☐ Previewing vocabulary
☐ Understanding new words: using punctuation clues
☐ Identifying the main ideas
☐ Understanding quotation marks
☐ Understanding new words from examples
☐ Identifying the topic and main idea of a paragraph
☐ Summarizing
☐ Creating passwords for websites

Target Vocabulary

Nouns
- categories (category)
- customers
- entertainment
- eye scan
- garage
- home improvement products
- information*
- Internet
- mall

- money*
- prediction
- products*
- profit
- purchases
- scientists*
- site
- stores*
- virtual shopping mall

Verbs
- choose*
- drove (drive)*
- predict
- put*
- quit
- search
- sell*
- socialize

Adjectives
- easy*
- gourmet
- huge*
- online
- second*

Adverb
- alone*

* These words are among the 1,000 most-frequently used words in English.

3 Friends and Family

"Any problem, big or small, within a family, always seems to start with bad communication. Someone isn't listening."

Emma Thompson
British actress

In Part 1, you will read and learn about new ways of staying connected with friends and family. In the rest of the chapter, you will read about, discuss and explore the positive and negative aspects of using technology for communication.

Connecting to the Topic

1. What do you see in the photo?

2. What are the people doing?

3. Name five ways that you communicate with friends and family.

New Ways of Staying Connected

Before You Read

1 **Thinking About the Topic** Look at the picture. Then answer these questions about it. Make a guess if you aren't sure.

Vocabulary Note

In different parts of the world, this has different names: **cell phone, mobile,** or **hand phone.** What do *you* call it?

1. What is each person doing?
2. How does each person feel?
3. Why do you think they feel this way?
4. Are you sometimes in this situation? Describe how it makes you feel.

2 **Interviewing Other Students** Look at the chart. Think about your answers to this question: How do you (your parents/your grandparents) usually communicate with friends and family? (Possible answers: *by letters, by email, on the phone, on a cell phone, by texting.*) Walk around the room with your book and a pencil and ask four students three questions. Write their answers in the chart on the next page. If a student doesn't know an answer, put a question mark (?).

Example

A: Sara, how do **you** usually communicate with friends and family?

B: I communicate with friends and family on Facebook and with Skype.

How do these people usually communicate with friends and family?			
Student's name	you	your parents	your grandparents
Sara	Facebook/Skype	Skype/email	cell phones/letters

In your chart, you have people from three age groups. Do they like to communicate in the same way or in different ways? Share your answers with the class.

 3 **Previewing Vocabulary** Read the words in the list. They are words from the next reading. Listen to their pronunciation. Do not look them up in a dictionary. Check (✓) the words that you don't know.

Nouns
- advice
- boss
- cons
- experts
- identity
- identity theft
- life issues

- pros
- screen
- smart phones
- social networking sites
- teenager

Verb
- stare

Adjectives
- dangerous
- face-to-face
- public
- shy

Strategy

Understanding New Words

You do not always need to use a dictionary to find the meaning of a new word.

- Sometimes pictures can help you to find the meaning of a new word. Look at the photo to the right. Read the caption. What do you think *stare* means? What does *screen* mean?

▲ Some people stare at a computer screen for many hours each day.

- Sometimes the words before *other* can help you with a new word.

We can invite friends to a party or other social event. (A party is an example of a social event.)

Understanding New Words: Using Pictures Before you read the next article, look at the photos and captions. Find words for these meanings. Write the words on the lines.

1. good points = _____pros_____

2. bad points = _____cons_____

3. in person, not online or on the phone = _____face - to - face_____

4. cell phone with computer features and email = _____smartphone_____

Strategy

Skimming

Skimming is the skill of reading quickly to understand the general ideas of a text. It is an important skill that good readers use every day.

You can skim a reading to identify the topic and main idea. When you skim, you can also try to predict or guess what the reading is about. Skimming a reading *before* you read it carefully can help you to better understand it. Follow these steps to skim:

- Read the title and any subheadings (titles of the parts).
- Look at photos and diagrams.
- Read the first and last line of each paragraph.
- Read quickly. Don't read every word.

 Skimming Before you read the article, skim it quickly to find only the answer to these questions. Don't write anything. Just think about the answers.

1. What is the title?

2. What are three subheadings?

3. Have a quick look at the photos in the article. Guess what the topic of the article is. Do you think it's an interesting topic?

6 **Reading an Article** Read the following article. Then do the activities.

New Ways of Staying Connected

Read # chorally

A How do we stay connected with friends and family? There are always letters, of course, or the telephone. But the Internet and **smart phones** are giving us new ways to connect with other people. These days, we can easily communicate with people on Facebook, Myspace, Twitter, and other **social networking sites**. Is this a good thing? Maybe not always. Social networking has both **pros** and **cons**.

5

Pros

What are the pros?

B Social networking is wonderful for friendships. We can use it to connect with people outside our neighborhood, anywhere in the world. We can socialize with family and old friends. We can make new friends.

10

▲ Pros: What's good about social networking?

▲ a smart phone

And with social networking, it's easy to invite friends to a party or other **social event**. Also, **shy** people (who have difficulty communicating in person) are often comfortable in a virtual friendship. They don't feel alone.

15

C Social networking sites can help with important **life issues** such as finding a job or finding a doctor or choosing a school. The sites offer ideas and **advice** from experts—people with a lot of information on a subject. Also, friends can help each other. For example, one person needs a new apartment. Another person is moving from his apartment soon. A friend of both people can connect them.

20

▲ Cons: What's bad about social networking?

Cons

D Social networking can be bad for friendships, too. Some people spend a lot of time online or on their smart phone. They **stare** for hours at the **screen**. They have virtual friendships, but they don't spend much **face-to-face** time with friends.

25

E Also, for several reasons, social networking can be dangerous. First, we don't always know the real **identity** of other people—who they really are. For example, a **teenager** thinks she is communicating with another teenage girl, but this person

30

▲ What's good about communication online or on a cell phone?
What's good about face-to-face communication?

is really a 40-year-old man. Is this really her "friend"? Second, information about us on a social networking site is **public**. Many, many people can see it. For example, at work, the **boss** can find personal information about employees. Some employees lose their jobs because of this. A very serious problem is **identity theft**, when people use public information to steal another person's identity. With another person's identity, they can steal money or get a passport, for example.

Conclusion

F   Social networking is changing the way we communicate with other people. It's now possible to communicate with almost anyone, almost anywhere. But it's important to be careful. If we're careful, there are more pros than cons with this new way of being connected.

Read chorally

After You Read

7 Identifying the Main Ideas Complete the sentences. Choose the best answer.

1. The main idea is that _____.

   Ⓐ there are many ways to communicate with other people

   Ⓑ social networking is changing the way we communicate

   Ⓒ social networking sites can help people to find a job or school

2. The writer thinks that _____.

   Ⓐ social networking is usually good because it's easy to communicate with anyone

   Ⓑ social networking is usually bad because it's dangerous

   Ⓒ there are more good things than bad things about social networking, if we're careful

On board

I
you
he
she
it
we
they
this
that
these
those

Def.

Understanding Pronouns

Pronouns are words such as *he, she, it, they, this, that, these,* or *those.* Pronouns take the place of nouns. Look before the pronoun to find the noun that it replaces. That will help you to understand the pronoun's meaning.

Examples

Some

I can't imagine life without my smart phone. I always have **it** with me.
(The word *it* refers to "smart phone.")

Shy people are often comfortable in a virtual friendship. **They** don't feel alone.
(The word *they* refers to "shy people.")

8 **Understanding Pronouns** Find the meaning of each underlined pronoun. Highlight the meaning of the pronoun. Then draw an arrow from the pronoun to its meaning.

1. Social networking is wonderful for friendships. We can use <u>it</u> to connect with people anywhere in the world.

2. Some people spend a lot of time online. <u>They</u> stare for hours at the screen.

3. We don't always know the real identity of other people—who <u>they</u> really are.

4. A teenager thinks <u>she</u> is communicating with another teenage girl, but this person is really a 40-year-old man.

5. Information about us on a social networking site is public. Many, many people can see <u>it</u>.

Group 1

9 **Identifying Vocabulary** Write the word or term for the meanings on the chart below. For help, look back at the blue words in the reading.

Meaning	Word or Term
Examples: Facebook, Google+, and Twitter	social networking sites
who a person is	identity
Examples: finding a job, finding a doctor, choosing a school	life issues
ideas, suggestions	advice
people with difficulty communicating in person	shy
a person between 13 and 19 years old	teenager
getting another person's information in order to steal	identity theft

Strategy

Recognizing Organization in an Essay
An essay has a main topic and a main idea. The topic of the first reading in this chapter is *social networking*. The main idea is that *social networking is changing the way we communicate with other people*. Many essays and articles are organized in this way:

- Paragraph A: Introduction of the topic and the main idea of the article or essay
- Paragraph B: Subtopic, main idea, and details
- Paragraph C: Another subtopic, main idea, and details
- Paragraph D: Another subtopic, main idea, and details
- Paragraph E: Another subtopic, main idea, and details
- Paragraph F: Conclusion (restates the main idea of the essay)

10 **Understanding Organization in an Essay: Using a Graphic Organizer** Fill in this graphic organizer with the topic and main idea of each paragraph of the reading on pages 43-44. Use your own words or copy from the reading.

Paragraph	Topic	Main Idea
A	social networking	Social networking has both pros and cons.
B	a pro of social networking	*Social networking is wonderful for friendships*
C	*another pro of social networking*	*It can help with life issues*
D	a con of social networking	*Social networking can be bad for friendships*
E	*another con of social networking*	*Social networking can be dangerous*
F	social networking	*There are more pros than cons but we must be careful*

11 **Thinking Critically** Discuss the following questions. Then share your answers with the class.

1. What's good about communication online or on a cell phone? Make a list.
2. What's good about face-to-face communication? Make a list.
3. In your opinion, are there more pros or cons to social networking?
4. Choose an example from your life to help explain your answer to #3.

Cell Phones Save Lives

Before You Read

1 Making Predictions Skim the title and photos in the next essay. Who are these people? What is happening in each picture? What do you think the essay is about?

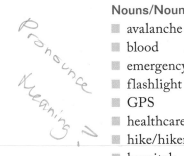

2 Previewing Vocabulary Read the words in the list. They are words from the next reading. Listen to their pronunciation. Do not look them up in a dictionary. Check (✓) the words that you don't know.

Nouns/Noun Phrases
- avalanche
- blood
- emergency
- flashlight
- GPS
- healthcare workers
- hike/hikers
- hospitals
- snow
- villages

Verbs/Verb Phrases
- find (found)
- get (got) lost
- save lives

Adjective
- pregnant

Adverb
- suddenly

Read

3 Reading an Essay Read the following essay quickly. As you read, use the pictures to help with new words. Then do the exercises.

Cell Phones Save Lives

A How do people use their cell phones? They can socialize: they talk with family and friends. They can use them for entertainment: they play games and watch movies. They use them as a video camera. They use them as an address book and to read their email. 5 Also, these days, people use cell phones to **save lives**.

B Many small **villages** in Rwanda, in Africa, are far from cities. There are no doctors or **hospitals**. What happens when a **pregnant** woman or new mother has a health problem? These days, the government is giving cell phones to 10 **healthcare workers**. They can call a doctor with their questions. The doctor gives them directions, and they can help the woman.

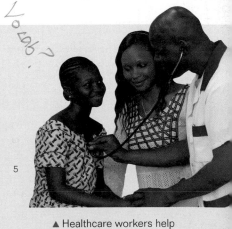

▲ Healthcare workers help a pregnant woman.

C   All over the world, people use cell phones in an **emergency**. A cell phone can be a **flashlight**. Some new cell phones can check a person's heart or **blood**. Some can send health information to and from the doctor. Also, many cell phones have a **GPS**. This helps emergency workers to **find** lost people.

15

20

▲ A cell phone can be used as a flashlight.

D   All **hikers** need a cell phone. It can save their lives. In New Zealand, for example, two tourists

▲ Why do hikers in the mountains need a cell phone?

from Taiwan were on a **hike** in the mountains. They **got** 25 **lost**. It was dark and raining. The National Park Police **found** them because of the GPS in their cell phones. In Washington State, in the United States, a hiker from Britain was on Granite Mountain. **Suddenly,** 30 there was an **avalanche**. The hiker was under many feet of **snow**. There, under the snow, he found his cell phone. He called 911. Emergency workers found him five hours later. 35

E   A cell phone is more than a phone. It lets us communicate with family and friends, of course. But in an emergency, it is also a real life saver.

What can you do in an avalanche? ▶

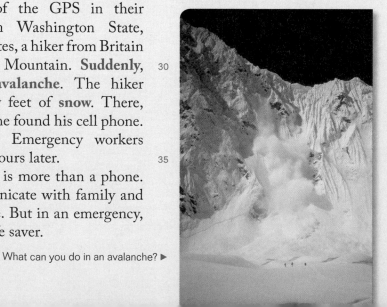

4 Identifying Main Ideas and Details Answer the following questions about the article. Choose the best answer for each.

1. In the writer's opinion, why is a cell phone more than just a phone?
   - (A) We can use it as entertainment.
   - (B) It can be a video camera.
   - (C) It can be a life saver.

2. How can cell phones save lives?
   - (A) People in small villages can communicate with doctors.
   - (B) People can call for help in an emergency.
   - (C) A and B

3. How does a GPS help people?
   - (A) It can be a flashlight.
   - (B) It helps emergency workers to find lost people.
   - (C) It sends health information to the doctor.

4. Why do hikers need a cell phone?
   - (A) The GPS can help them if they get lost.
   - (B) They can use it as a video camera.
   - (C) They can tell their friends about their hike in the mountains.

FOCUS

Using a Print Dictionary—Alphabetical Order

Sometimes you need to use a print dictionary. The words in a dictionary are in alphabetical order from—A to Z. It's important to know how to alphabetize quickly. Look at the first letter of each word to put words in alphabetical order.

These words are in alphabetical order.

advice

life

work

If the first letter is the same, you need to look at the second letter, too.

category

cons

customer

If the first and second letters are the same, you need to look at the third letter, and so on.

coffee

cola

company

5 Using a Print Dictionary—Alphabetical Order Put the words in alphabetical order by numbering them. The first word is 1; the second word is 2, and so on.

7	expert	5	entertainment	6	exercise
3	easy	12	hot	10	home
	hospital	16	networking	13	identity
4	emergency	22	village	18	public
21	suddenly	17	pregnant	15	issues
8	health	1	avalanche	2	dangerous
9	help	20	smart	23	virtual
14	information	19	scientist		

Using the Internet

Using the Internet as a Dictionary Tool
Another way to look new words up is to go online and use a search engine like Google. In the search box, type the new word + *definition* + *ESL*.

Example:

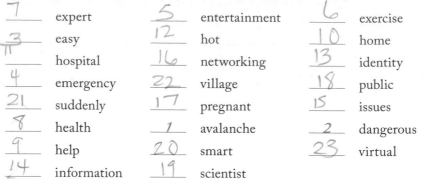

```
shadow definition ESL              |  Submit
```

Search Results
- **Shadow - Definition** and More from the Free Merriam-Webster...
  Definition of **shadow** from the Merriam-Webster Online Dictionary with audio pronunciations, thesaurus, Word of the Day, and word games.
  www.merriam-webster.com/dictionary/shadow - Cached - Similar
- Commonly Confused Words for **ESL** Students - Part II
  shadow: the dark area created by something else on a sunny day.
  esl.about.com/cs/vocabulary/a/a_confused_2.htm - Cached - Similar
- afraid of one's own **shadow** | **definition** by Idiom Quest
  Translate the **meaning** of the phrase afraid of one's own **shadow** to your target... Advanced Learners of English in Business and Academia - TOEFL / **ESL** / EFL...
  www.idiomquest.com/learn/idiom/afraid-of-one's-own-shadow/ - Cached - Similar

Click on one of these online dictionaries. If you don't understand the definition of your word, click on another online dictionary.

6 Researching Words Now go back to the readings that begin on pages 43 and 47. Circle any words that you don't know. Look for them in a print or online dictionary. Write their definitions.

7 **Writing in Your Journal** Choose one topic below. Write about it for five minutes. Use some of the vocabulary that you have learned in this chapter.

- What are pros (or cons) of social networking sites, in your opinion?
- What is your favorite social networking site, and why?
- How do you use your cell phone? Write all the ways.

<table>
<tr><td>PART</td><td>3</td><td>Practical English</td></tr>
</table>

Web log

1 **Reading a Blog** Writing for blogs is often more informal than other writing. It's closer to spoken English. Read this blog about cell phones.

Read
Vocb

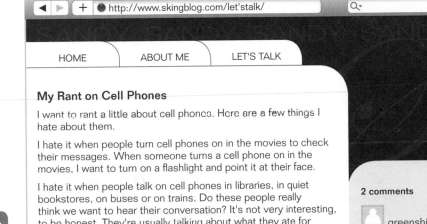

�,◀ ▶ + ● http://www.skingblog.com/let'stalk/

| HOME | ABOUT ME | LET'S TALK |

My Rant on Cell Phones

I want to rant a little about cell phones. Here are a few things I hate about them.

I hate it when people turn cell phones on in the movies to check their messages. When someone turns a cell phone on in the movies, I want to turn on a flashlight and point it at their face.

I hate it when people talk on cell phones in libraries, in quiet bookstores, on buses or on trains. Do these people really think we want to hear their conversation? It's not very interesting, to be honest. They're usually talking about what they ate for breakfast, and we can't hear the other end of the conversation (although I'm pretty sure the other side of the conversation is just as boring).

I hate it when people answer their phone calls while I'm talking to them, and then, in front of me, continue a long conversation. I also hate it when people text while I'm sitting at dinner with them. This is probably the worst thing people do on cell phones. This sends the message to the person you are eating with that "You are not interesting or important enough. I'd rather text my other friend. Obviously, I like this other friend much better than I like you."

I saw a girl yesterday standing in front of the Pacific Ocean. The sun was setting. The sky was pink, purple, orange, and blue. The waves were rolling onto the beach. She was looking down at her little pink cell phone, texting something. She did not look up once. I wanted to tell her to throw that cell phone in the ocean and start to enjoy the wonderful world in front of her.

Posted by Sandy King at 3:19 PM

Email This Blog! Share to Twitter Share to Facebook Share to Google Buzz

2 comments

greenships said...

I work at a fast-food restaurant and I really hate it when people don't get off their phone for the thirty seconds it takes to order a hamburger. Do they realize I am a human being?

July 10, 3:41 PM

mariangeorge said...

Relax. Cell phones are a part of our lives. Why don't you worry about important things like world peace or hunger?

July 10, 3:42 PM

Vocabulary Tip

A **rant** is an angry written or spoken text. **Rant** is also a verb, as in, "He was **ranting** about cell phones."

Texting is using your phone to send written messages.

2 **Understanding What You Read** Choose the correct answers below.

1. People usually rant about _____.

    Ⓐ things that make them happy

    Ⓑ things that make them sad

    Ⓒ things that make them angry

2. According to the writer, the worst thing that people do with cell phones is _____.

    Ⓐ text someone at the beach

    Ⓑ text someone while they are eating dinner with someone else

    Ⓒ text someone in a library

3. The writer probably _____.

    Ⓐ answers her cell phone when at dinner

    Ⓑ hates people who have cell phones

    Ⓒ tries to use her cell phone politely

4. The writer _____.

    Ⓐ is going to turn a flashlight on in the movies

    Ⓑ would like to turn a flashlight on in the movies

    Ⓒ does not like people who use flashlights

 3 **Discussing Cell Phone Use** In a small group, discuss the use of cell phones.

1. Look at the comments on the blog on page 51. Do you agree with Sandy King and "greenships" or with "mariangeorge"?

2. Tell your group a story about your experience with cell phone use.

3. Write a comment about the blog post in the comment box below. Discuss your comment with the class.

> **Comment**

---

1 **Practicing New Words** Use the words in the box to complete the paragraph on the next page.

cell phones	lost	hike	saved	mountains
emergency	called	cold	snowing	lives

George and Alex were on a _____hike_____ in the _mountains_. The day suddenly got _____cold_____ and it began _Showing_. They looked around, but they couldn't see anything. They were _____lost_____. Then they remembered they had their _cell phones_. They _____called_____ 911 and reached _emergency_ help. Their cell phones probably _Saved_ their _____lives_____ that day.

2 **Building Vocabulary** Below are words from this chapter. Circle the word that does not belong in each group.

1. pro   issue   (screen)   con
2. snow   (blog)   hiker   avalanche
3. emergency   (con)   save   911
4. rant   worry   angry   (text)

3 **Listening: Focusing on High-Frequency Words** Listen and fill in each blank with a word from the box. Some of the words are new, and some are not new.

alone	event	friendship	person
anywhere	family	invite	virtual
connect	friends	make	

Social networking is wonderful for _friendships_. We can use it to _connect_ with people outside our neighborhood, _anywhere_ in the world. We can socialize with _family_ and old _friends_. We can _make_ new friends. And with social networking, it's easy to _invite_ friends to a party or other social _event_. Also, shy people (who have difficulty communicating in _person_) are often comfortable in a _virtual_ friendship. They don't feel _alone_.

4 Writing Sentences with New Vocabulary Use these words from Chapter 3 to make your own sentences.

1. use/cell phones *People use cell phones in many different ways. They use email. They make phone calls. They even use a cell phone as a flashlight.*

2. hikers/cell phone _____

   _____

3. steal/identity _____

   _____

4. check/heart _____

   _____

5. I hate it when people… _____

5 Building Vocabulary Complete the crossword puzzle with words from the box. These words are from Chapter 3.

advice	dangerous	pros	theft
avalanche	emergency	rant	tourist
blood	expert	shy	village
boss	hike	stare	
cons	pregnant	teenager	

Across

1. walking trip (n)

5. red liquid in your body (n)

8. a person thirteen to nineteen years old (n)

10. a small town (n)

11. the stealing of something (n.)

15. important person at work (n)

17. reasons against (n.)

18. big problem (n)

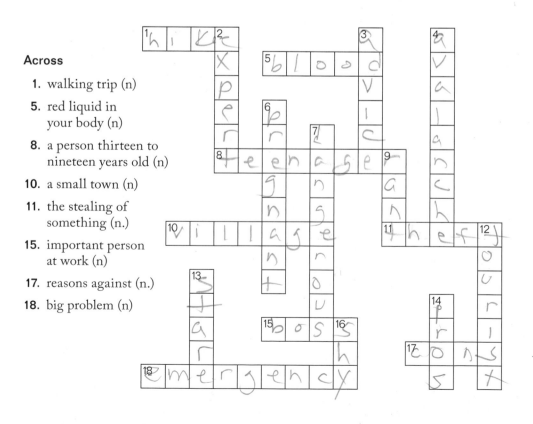

Down

2. someone who knows (n)
3. information to help someone (n)
4. snow problem (n)
6. going to have a baby (adj.)
7. not safe (adj.)

9. angry text or speech (n)
12. traveler (n)
13. look at for a long time (v.)
14. reasons for (n.)
16. not comfortable in groups (adj.)

Self-Assessment Log

Read the lists below. Check (✓) the strategies and vocabulary that you learned in this chapter. Look through the chapter or ask your instructor about the strategies and words that you do not understand.

Reading and Vocabulary-Building Strategies

☐ Understanding new words: using a dictionary
☐ Skimming a reading
☐ Understanding pronouns
☐ Recognizing organization in an essay
☐ Putting words in alphabetical order
☐ Using the Internet as a dictionary tool

Target Vocabulary

Nouns
- advice
- avalanche
- blood*
- boss
- cons
- emergency
- flashlight
- GPS
- healthcare workers
- hike/hikers
- hospitals
- identity

- identity theft
- life issues
- pros
- screen
- smart phones
- snow
- social networking sites
- teenager
- villages*

Verbs
- find* (found)
- get (got) lost
- save lives
- stare

Adjectives
- dangerous
- face-to-face
- pregnant
- public
- shy

Adverb
- suddenly*

* These words are among the 1,000 most frequently used words in English.

4 Health Care

"Prevention is better
than cure."

Desiderius Erasmus
Dutch humanist and theologian

In this
CHAPTER

In Part 1, you will read about foods, drinks, and lifestyles that will help you stay physically and mentally healthy. In the rest of this chapter, you will read about, explore, and discuss issues about health, the body, and going to the doctor.

Connecting to the Topic

1. What is the woman doing? What are the other people doing?

2. Why are they doing these things? Are these things healthy?

3. What are five healthy things that people do? What are five unhealthy things that people often do?

Health News for Body and Mind

Before You Read

1 Thinking About the Topic Look at this chart. Which things are good for your health? Which are bad? Check (✓) *Good* or *Bad* in one of the first two columns.

Then make another decision. Are they good for your physical health (your body) or your mental health? Check (✓) *Physical Health*, *Mental Health*, both, or neither.

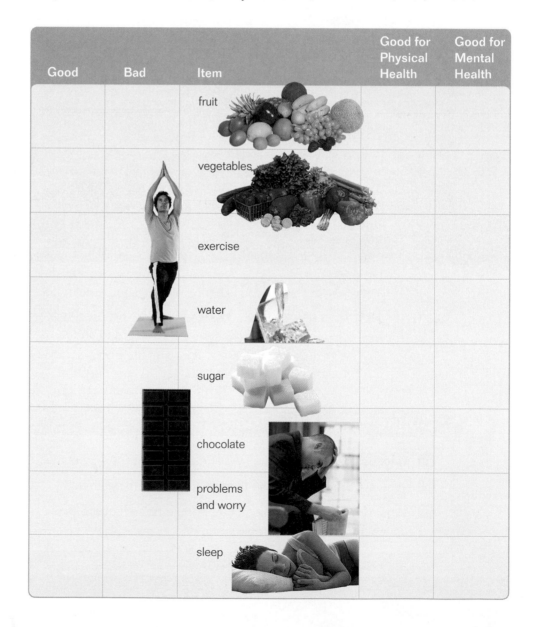

Good	Bad	Item	Good for Physical Health	Good for Mental Health
		fruit		
		vegetables		
		exercise		
		water		
		sugar		
		chocolate		
		problems and worry		
		sleep		

2 **Comparing Answers** Show your chart to other students. Are your answers the same? Which answers are different? Why do you think this may be?

3 **Previewing Vocabulary** Read the words below. Listen to their pronunciation. Do not look them up in a dictionary. Put a check mark (✓) next to the words that you don't know.

Nouns
- antioxidants
- beverages
- blood pressure
- body
- brain
- calcium
- cocoa
- couch potato
- diseases

- DNA
- junk food
- sleep
- stress
- university
- wrinkles

Verbs
- age
- damage

- sleep
- smoke
- solves

Adjectives
- bilingual
- chronic
- difficult
- healthy
- mental

- physical
- sleep-deprived
- surprising

Adverb
- often

Strategy

Finding Meaning After *Which* or *Who*
You do not always need to use a dictionary to find the meaning of a new word. Sometimes the meaning of a new word comes after a comma and the word *which* or *who*.

Example

Too much **stress**,　which is worry about problems in life,　is not good for your physical health.

A **dentist**,　who takes care of people's teeth,　has an interesting profession.

4 **Finding Meaning After *Which* or *Who*** The meanings of the words in the box below are in the next reading. Find the words and circle their meanings.

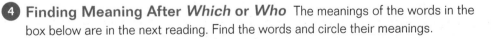

| bilingual | chronic | sleep-deprived |

Read

5 **Reading an Article** Read the following article. Don't use your dictionary. If you don't know some words, try to figure out their meanings. Then do the activities.

Health News for Body and Mind

A Nobody wants to be **sick**. Everyone wants to be **healthy**, and most people want to have a long life, too. But a healthy **body** is not enough. We all want both **physical** and **mental** health. What can we do to stay well? Most of us know some things to do. It's a good idea to exercise (for example, in a gym), eat fruit, vegetables, and fish, and drink lots of water. We also know things *not* to do; it's a bad idea to eat a lot of **junk food**, such as chips, ice cream, candy, donuts, and other foods with sugar or fat. It's a bad idea to be a **couch potato**—a person who watches a lot of TV and doesn't exercise. It's a terrible idea to **smoke**. But scientists now have new information about *other* ways to stay healthy. Some of it is **surprising**.

Drink Cocoa

B Several **beverages** are good for the health. Orange juice has vitamin C. Milk has **calcium**. Black tea and green tea are good for health, too. They have **antioxidants**; these fight **diseases** such as cancer and heart disease. Most people know this. But most people *don't* know about **cocoa**—hot chocolate. They enjoy the sweet, chocolaty beverage, but they don't know about its antioxidants. It has more antioxidants than tea!

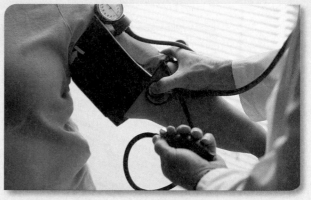

▲ High blood pressure is bad for your health. (Normal blood pressure is 120/80.)

Relax

C Too much **stress**, which is worry about problems in life, is not good for physical health. For example, it makes your **blood pressure** go up. Now we know more. Some stress is **chronic,** which means that it lasts a long time—for many months or years. Chronic stress can make people old. As people get older, they get gray hair and **wrinkles** in their skin, and their eyesight and hearing become worse. This is normal. But chronic stress makes people **age**—grow old—*faster*. A scientist at the University of California, San Francisco, studies stress. She can now identify *how* stress makes people age. It can **damage** (hurt) the body's **DNA**. The lesson from this is clear. We need to learn to relax.

◄ A model of DNA

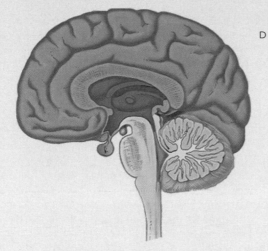

▲ The brain **solves** problems during sleep.

Sleep

D   One easy and cheap way to help both your physical and mental health is just to sleep eight hours or more every night, but more and more people are not sleeping enough. According to the World Health Organization, over half the people in the world may be **sleep-deprived**, which means they don't get enough sleep. Sleep-deprived people often have medical problems, such as high blood pressure, diabetes (a problem with sugar in the blood), and heart problems. It is also more **difficult** for them to make decisions. Clearly, we need to find time to get more sleep. But there is another reason. A new study from Germany found that sleep makes people *smarter*. The study shows that the **brain** continues to work during sleep and helps the sleeper to work on problems. You didn't do your homework last night? Maybe you can tell your teacher that you were working hard in your sleep!

Learn Languages

E   How many languages do you speak? There might be good news for you. A study from a **university** in Canada found something interesting. **Bilingual** people, who speak two languages very well, do better on tests than people who speak only one language. It seems to be mental "exercise" to hold two languages in your brain. Ellen Bialystok of York University says it's "like going to a brain gym."

Conclusion

F   To have good physical and mental health, we need to eat right, relax, sleep enough, and exercise (both the body and the brain). There is a lot of new information about health. Some of it is surprising. We need to know about it.

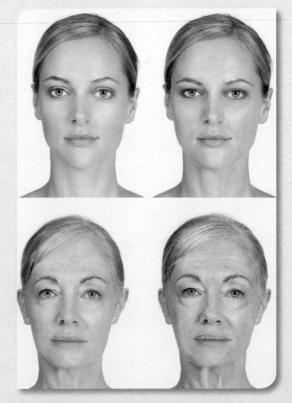

▲ Gray hair and wrinkles are natural effects of aging.

6 Understanding Main Ideas According to the reading, what is good for your health? Write *G* for *Good*. What is bad for your health? Write *B* for *Bad*.

1. _G_ cocoa
2. _B_ stress
3. _G_ sleep
4. _G_ speaking two languages

7 Identifying Vocabulary Write the word or term for the definitions below. For help, look back at the boldfaced words in the reading.

	Definition	Word or Term
1.	person who watches a lot of TV and doesn't exercise	couch potato
2.	examples: chips, ice cream, candy, donuts, and other foods with sugar or fat	junk food
3.	something in milk that is good for the health	calcium
4.	example: cancer	diseases
5.	problems and worry about your life	stress
6.	lasting a long time (months or years)	chronic
7.	get old	age
8.	without enough sleep	sleep-deprived
9.	speaking two languages	bilingual

8 Finding Important Details Work with classmates to fill in a chart like this with information from Paragraphs B–E. How many details can you find?

What is good for your health?	Why?
orange juice	It has vitamin C.
What is bad for your health?	**Why?**

9 Understanding Pronouns Find and highlight the meaning of each underlined pronoun. Then draw an arrow from the pronoun to its meaning.

1. Many people don't know about cocoa. It has more antioxidants than tea.

2. They have antioxidants; these fight diseases.

3. Some stress is chronic, which means it lasts a long time.

4. A scientist at the University of California studies stress. She can now identify how stress makes people age.

5. Green tea and black tea are good for the health. They have antioxidants.

Strategy

Understanding Italics
Italics are slanted letters, *like these*. Writers use them for different reasons. One reason is for words that are important. When people read out loud, these words sound a little louder and higher than other words.

10 Understanding Italics Go back to the reading. How many words can you find in italics? Read those sentences out loud to a partner.

FOCUS

Changing Nouns to Adjectives
Sometimes we can change a noun to an adjective by adding a *-y* to the singular form of the noun. For example, to change the noun *health* into an adjective, we add a *-y*. *Healthy* means "in good health."

Example

She's in good **health**. (noun)

She's a **healthy** person. (adjective)

If the noun ends in a vowel, you have to drop the vowel before adding *-y.*

Example

I love **chocolate**. (noun)

I love this **chocolaty** dessert. (adjective)

11 Changing Nouns to Adjectives Complete the following sentences with the appropriate adjective. Change a noun in the sentence to an adjective.

1. If a person is very smart (has a good *brain*), she is ____brainy____.

2. If you have a lot of luck, you are ____lucky____.

3. If something has a lot of dirt, it's ___dirty___.

4. If you need sleep, you are ___sleepy___.

5. A drink is cold because it has ice in it. It is an ___icy___ drink.

 12 Discussing the Reading Discuss the following questions in a small group.

1. According to new studies, what diseases can cocoa fight?

2. What can you do to age more slowly?

3. What can you do to be smarter?

Are You Healthy?

Before You Read

1 Making Predictions Before you do the questionnaire in Activity 3, answer this question:

How is your health? Check (✓) one.

___✓___ great ___ good ___ okay ___ bad ___ terrible

 2 Previewing Vocabulary Read the words below. Listen to their pronunciation. Do not look them up in a dictionary. Put a check mark (✓) next to the words that you don't know.

Nouns
- alcohol
- breakfast
- cigarettes
- pounds

Adjective
- overweight

Adverbs
- never
- seldom

- sometimes
- usually

Read

 3 Reading and Answering a Questionnaire Read the questions in the questionnaire on the next page. Choose your answers. This will help you to answer the question, "Am I healthy?"

Am I Healthy?

1. Do you eat a healthful breakfast every day?

   3
   - (A) yes
   - (B) usually
   - (C) no

2. Do you eat fruits and vegetables every day?

   3
   - (A) yes, 5 or more
   - (B) yes, 1 or 2
   - (C) no

3. Do you smoke?

   3
   - (A) never
   - (B) yes, 1–10 cigarettes every day
   - (C) yes, more than 10 cigarettes every day

4. Do you drink cola?

   3
   - (A) no
   - (B) yes, 1–2 glasses every day
   - (C) yes, 3–10 glasses every day

5. Do you eat junk food?

   5
   - (A) never
   - (B) sometimes
   - (C) often

6. How much do you sleep every night?

   - (A) 8–9 hours
   - (B) 6–7 hours
   - (C) 3–5 hours

   2

7. Are you overweight?

   3
   - (A) no
   - (B) yes, 5–19 pounds
   - (C) yes, 20–50 pounds

8. How much stress do you have?

   - (A) very little
   - (B) some
   - (C) a lot, every day

   0

9. How far do you walk every day?

   - (A) 1–5 miles
   - (B) ½ –1 mile
   - (C) 0 miles

   2

10. How often do you exercise?

    3
    - (A) often
    - (B) 1 time every week
    - (C) seldom or never

11. How much alcohol (beverages like beer and wine) do you drink every week?

    - (A) 0–2 glasses
    - (B) 3–5 glasses
    - (C) 6 or more glasses

    5

12. Do you worry, or are you unhappy?

    - (A) seldom
    - (B) sometimes
    - (C) often

    2

Do you eat junk food? ▶

Next, add up your score.

   Every answer *a* = 3 points.

   Every answer *b* = 2 points.

   Every answer *c* = 0 points.

YOUR SCORE: _____

Am I healthy?

   30–36 points = You're probably very healthy.

   25–29 points = You might need to make some changes.

   0–24 points = You might not be very healthy.

Culture Note

Smoking

In some countries, people are trying to quit smoking. In other countries, more people (especially young people) are starting to smoke. What is the situation like where you live? What is the situation like in another country that you know well?

After You Read

FOCUS

Giving Advice

To give another person advice, you can use the modal *should*.

should ———┐
          ├——— + the simple form of the verb
should not ———┘

Example

You **shouldn't worry** so much. You **should try** to relax.

4 Discussing the Reading: Giving Advice Work with a partner. Look at your partner's answers to the questions on the health test. Give your partner advice. Use *should* and *shouldn't*.

Examples

You should eat a good breakfast every day.

You shouldn't eat so much junk food.

Using a Dictionary—Guide Words

Sometimes you can't understand a new word without a dictionary. If you want to find a word fast, you need to use guide words. Guide words are at the top of every dictionary page, usually in the left and right corners.

Example

Look at the dictionary page below. The guide words are *picnic* and *pig*. The first word on this page is *picnic*. The last word is *pig*. The words are in alphabetical order between these two guide words. Look at the guide words, and you'll know if your new word is on this page.

picnic	386	pig

picnic (4) [pik'nik], *n.* a meal planned for eating outdoors. **Ex.** *They ate their picnic beside the river.* —*v.* have a picnic. **Ex.** *We picnicked in the woods.* —**pic'nick·er**, *n.* **Ex.** *After lunch, the picnickers made up teams for a game of baseball.*

picture (1) [pik'čər], *n.* 1. a painting, drawing, or photograph. **Ex.** *That picture of the President is seen often in the newspaper.* 2. that which strongly resembles another; an image. **Ex.** *She is the picture of her mother.* 3. a description. **Ex.** *The author gives a lively picture of his life as a sailor.* 4. a motion picture; movie. **Ex.** *The whole family enjoyed the picture we saw last night.* —*v.* describe. **Ex.** *The speaker pictured the scene in colorful words.* —**pic·tor'i·al**, *adj.*

pie (2) [pay'], *n.* a baked dish consisting of a thin shell, and sometimes a cover, made of flour and cooking oil and filled with fruit, meat, etc. **Ex.** *She put the pie in the oven to bake.*

piece (1) [piys'], *n.* 1. an amount or a part considered as an individual unit. **Ex.** *Please give me a piece of writing paper.* 2. a part taken away from something larger. **Ex.** *She cut the pie into six pieces.* 3. a coin. **Ex.** *Can you change this fifty-cent piece?* —*v.* join together; make whole. **Ex.** *She pieced together the broken dish.* —**go to pieces**, become upset or excited. **Ex.** *He goes to pieces when I disagree with him.*

piecemeal [piys'miyl'], *adv.* one part at a time; piece by piece. **Ex.** *He put the machine together piecemeal in his spare time.*

piecework [piys'wərk'], *n.* work paid for by the piece finished instead of by the hour, day, etc. **Ex.** *She does piecework at home.*

pier (3) [pi:r'], *n.* a structure built over the water and used as a landing place for ships and boats. **Ex.** *The ship is at pier seven.*

pierce (4) [pirs'], *v.* 1. break into or through. **Ex.** *The knife had pierced the wall.* 2. make a hole or opening in. **Ex.** *Many girls have their ears pierced for earrings.* 3. force a way through. **Ex.** *They tried to pierce the enemy's defense.* 4. deeply or sharply affect the senses or feelings. **Ex.** *They were pierced by the icy winds.*

pig (2) [pig'], *n.* a farm animal with a broad nose and fat body, raised for its meat.

5 **Using a Dictionary—Guide Words** Use your dictionary. Find the following pages quickly. What are the guide words? Write them on the blanks. If there are no guide words, write the first and last words on the page.

1. page 32 _____ _____

2. page 196 _____ _____

3. page 15 _____ _____

4. page 203 _____ _____

5. page 78 _____ _____

6 **Understanding Guide Words** Read the vocabulary words and the guide words below. For each word answer this question: *Could you find this vocabulary word between the guide words?* Write *yes* or *no* on each line below.

Vocabulary Words		**Guide Words**
1. _no_	speak	sleep–smoke
2. _yes_	beverage	bed–big
3. _yes_	new	never–night
4. _no_	mental	most–mother
5. _no_	overweight	old–only
6. _no_	damage	dance–difficult
7. _yes_	solve	sick–sometimes
8. _no_	wrinkle	walk–weight

7 **Using a Dictionary** Find these words in your dictionary. Use the guide words in the dictionary for help. Write the page number and the guide words for each word.

Word	Page	Guide Words	Word	Page	Guide Words
elbow			cough		
headache			throat		
stomach			thumb		
pain			cold		

8 **Writing in Your Journal** Choose one topic below. Write about it for five minutes. Use some of the vocabulary that you have learned in this chapter.

- things that you do that are good for your health
- something that you do that is not good for your health
- something that you learned about health in this chapter

Going to the Doctor

1 **Identifying Body Parts** Read the body parts in the box. Then read the sentences and look at the picture. Write the body part in each blank and next to the correct number in the picture.

ankle	elbow	head	nose
~~chest~~	~~eyes~~	hip	shoulder
chin	fingers	knee	toes
ears	foot	neck	wrist

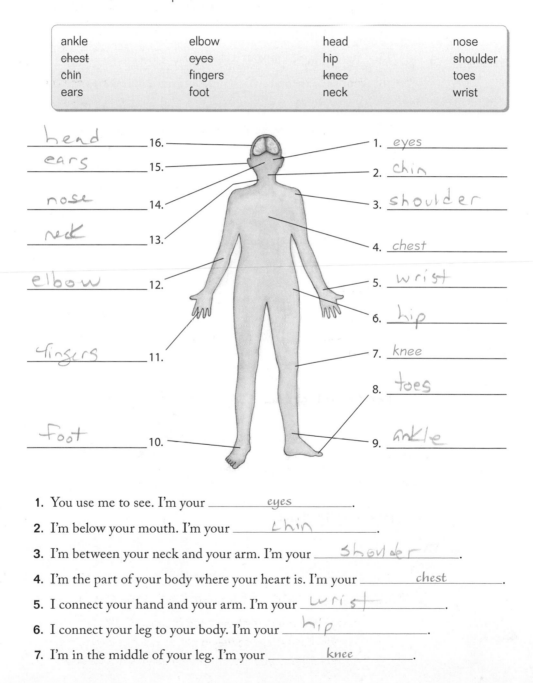

head 16.

ears 15.

nose 14.

neck 13.

elbow 12.

fingers 11.

foot 10.

1. _eyes_

2. _chin_

3. _shoulder_

4. _chest_

5. _wrist_

6. _hip_

7. _knee_

8. _toes_

9. _ankle_

1. You use me to see. I'm your _____ _eyes_ _____.

2. I'm below your mouth. I'm your _____ _chin_ _____.

3. I'm between your neck and your arm. I'm your _____ _shoulder_ _____.

4. I'm the part of your body where your heart is. I'm your _____ _chest_ _____.

5. I connect your hand and your arm. I'm your _____ _wrist_ _____.

6. I connect your leg to your body. I'm your _____ _hip_ _____.

7. I'm in the middle of your leg. I'm your _____ _knee_ _____.

8. There are ten of me—five on each foot. I'm your _toes_.

9. I connect your foot and your leg. I'm your _ankle_.

10. Five toes are on me. I'm your _foot_.

11. You have ten of me on your hands, and they help you write. I'm your _fingers_.

12. I'm in the middle of your arm. I'm your _elbow_.

13. I connect your head to your body. I'm your _neck_.

14. I smell things. I'm your _nose_.

15. I hear things. I'm your _ears_.

16. Your ears are on my right and left sides. I'm your _head_.

2 **Identifying Body Parts: On The Inside** Look at the picture of the body. Then look at the words in the box. Write the names of the body parts on the blank lines. If you don't know the names, you can look in a dictionary.

brain	kidneys	lungs	stomach
heart	large intestine	small intestine	throat

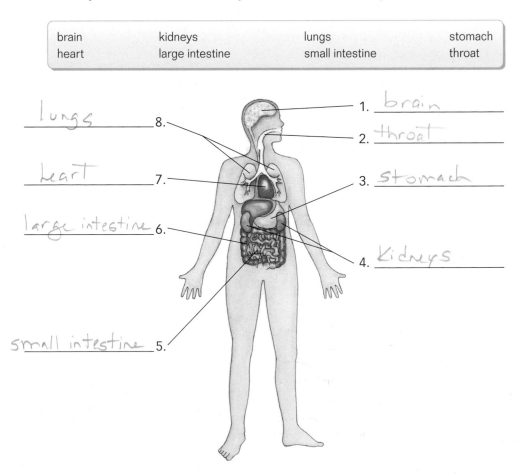

lungs 8.

heart 7.

large intestine 6.

small intestine 5.

1. _brain_

2. _throat_

3. _stomach_

4. _kidneys_

Describing Illnesses

Sometimes people get sick. Here are some illnesses that people sometimes have.

a headache.

a cough.

I have —

a broken arm.

a stomachache.

a cold.

3 **Describing Illnesses** Look at the photo to the right. What do you think the people are saying to each other? Work with a partner and write a short conversation. The doctor can ask questions like these: "How are you feeling?" or "What's wrong?" The patient can answer by completing this sentence: "I have _____."

"How are you feeling?" ▶

Matching Meaning We use the word *heart* in many expressions in English. Can you guess the meaning of the expressions below? Put the letter of the meaning that matches the expression on the blank.

1. __c__ The museum is right *in the heart of* the new downtown.

2. __a__ His wife asked for a divorce. *His heart is breaking.*

3. __b__ *A heart attack* is a very serious medical emergency.

4. __h__ She never liked fish before, but now she loves fish. She had *a change of heart* about fish.

5. __f__ I love you. You *make my heart sing.*

6. __g__ He doesn't like anyone. He *has a cold heart.*

7. __e__ In this argument, *in your heart of hearts*, you know I'm right.

8. __d__ My grandmother loves to play with children. She's really a kid *at heart*.

a. He is very sad.

b. a problem with your heart

c. in the middle of

d. the way she feels inside, not the way she looks on the outside

e. in your true feelings

f. give me happiness

g. is unfriendly or without feelings

h. a new feeling or idea

PART 4 Vocabulary Practice

---

1 **Building Vocabulary** Read the words in each row below. Which word does not fit? Circle it.

1. beverage	tea	cocoa	(blood)
2. headache	pain	(healthy)	disease
3. brain	(foot)	kidneys	heart
4. pounds	(usually)	overweight	food
5. sometimes	(chronic)	seldom	never
6. alcohol	drink	(eat)	wine
7. (never)	usually	often	daily
8. lungs	cigarettes	(sleep)	smoke
9. stomachache	(wrinkle)	pain	sick

2 **Identifying Opposites** Draw a line to the word that has the opposite meaning.

1. small
2. healthy
3. new
4. overweight
5. stress
6. never
7. breakfast
8. university
9. mental
10. difficult
11. sleep

a. old
b. relaxation
c. underweight
d. wake
e. kindergarten
f. easy
g. sick
h. large
i. physical
j. always
k. dinner

3 **Listening: Focusing on High-Frequency Words** Listen and fill in the words you hear.

How many _languages_ do you speak? There might be good news
for you. A study from a _university_ in Canada found something
interesting. _Bilingual_ people, who speak two languages very well,
do better on tests than people who _speak_ only one language.
It seems to be _mental_ "exercise" to hold two languages in
your brain. Ellen Bialystok of York University says it's "like going to a
brain gym."

To have good physical and mental health, we need to _eat_
right, relax, _sleep_ enough, and _exercise_ (both the
body and the brain). There is a lot of new information about
health. Some of it is _surprising_. We need to know about it.

4 **Building Vocabulary** Complete the crossword puzzle. These words are from Chapter 4.

age	cocoa	junk food	solve
beverages	damage	kidneys	stomach
chest	diseases	mental	stress
chin	healthy	never	wrinkles
chronic	intestine	sick	

Across

4. worry (n.)
6. hurt, harm, or break something (v.)
9. lines on your skin (n.)
11. drinks of all kinds (n.)
12. Your heart is inside this. (n.)
16. unhealthful things to eat (two words) (n.)
18. always there; lasting a long time (adj.)
19. When you do this to a problem, the problem is fixed. (v.)

Down

1. cancer, AIDS, heart problems, diabetes (n.)
2. not even once (adv.)
3. opposite of sick (adj.)
5. opposite of healthy (adj.)
7. get older (v.)
8. You have both a large and a small one of these. (n.)
10. a hot chocolate drink (n.)
13. where your food goes first when you eat (n.)
14. There are two of these, on the right and left, near your stomach. (n.)
15. happening in the mind (adj.)
17. This is below your mouth. (n.)

Self-Assessment Log

Read the lists below. Check (✓) the strategies and vocabulary that you learned in this chapter. Look through the chapter or ask your instructor about the strategies and words that you do not understand.

Reading and Vocabulary-Building Strategies

- ☐ Finding meaning after *which* or *who*
- ☐ Identifying vocabulary
- ☐ Finding important details
- ☐ Understanding pronouns
- ☐ Understanding italics
- ☐ Changing nouns to adjectives
- ☐ Giving advice
- ☐ Using a dictionary: understanding guide words
- ☐ Identifying body parts
- ☐ Describing illnesses
- ☐ Identifying opposites

Target Vocabulary

Nouns

- alcohol
- ankle
- beverages
- blood pressure
- body*
- brain
- breakfast
- calcium
- chest
- chin
- cigarettes
- cocoa
- couch potato
- cough
- diseases
- ears*
- elbow
- eyes*

- fingers*
- foot*
- head*
- heart*
- hip
- junk food
- kidneys
- knee
- large intestine
- lungs
- mouth*
- neck
- nose
- pounds*
- shoulder*
- sleep*
- small intestine
- stomach
- stress

- throat
- toes
- university
- wrinkles
- wrist

Verbs

- age*
- damage
- should*
- sleep*
- smoke
- solves

Adjectives

- bilingual
- chronic
- difficult*
- healthy

- mental
- overweight
- physical
- sleep-deprived
- surprising

Adverbs

- never*
- often*
- seldom
- sometimes*
- usually*

*These words are among the 1,000 most-frequently used words in English.

CHAPTER 5

Men and Women

"No matter your job
or your workplace,
dealing with people
effectively is a
must for success."

Susan M. Heathfield
Human resources expert,
speaker, and trainer

In Part 1, you will read about the different ways in which men and women do business. In the rest of this chapter, you will read about, explore, and discuss how young men and women communicate on college campuses.

Connecting to the Topic

1. What relationships do these people have with each other?

2. What are the people doing? How are they communicating?

3. List three possible problems that people have with each other at work.

Men and Women in Business

Before You Read

1 **Interviewing Other Students** Look at the chart below. Walk around the room and ask as many students as possible the three questions below. Write their answers in this chart. For Questions 1 and 2, use symbols to show the number of people who gave each answer. For example, || = 2 people, ||||| = 5 people. For Question 3, write your classmates' answers in words.

Question 1	Men's Answers		Women's Answers	
Is it important to have a high position at work?	Yes	No	Yes	No

Question 2	Men's Answers		Women's Answers	
When you have a problem at school or work, what do you like to do?	I usually solve it myself.	I usually ask for help.	I usually solve it myself.	I usually ask for help.

Question 3	Men's Answers	Women's Answers
What does it mean when a person **nods** (moves the head up and down)?		

2 **Critical Thinking: Understanding a Graph** Look at the graph on page 79. Then discuss the following questions.

1. Which field has more women? About what percent (%) are women? About what percent are men?

2. Which field has more men? About what percent are men? Women?

3. Which field has an almost equal (same) number of women and men?

4. This graph is about college graduates in the United States in 2008. Do you think the numbers are different today? Are the numbers different in other countries?

Men and Women in Three Fields: Engineering, Education, and Business

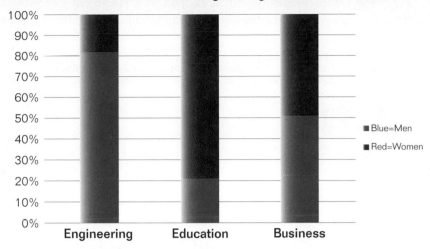

■ Blue=Men
■ Red=Women

3 **Previewing Vocabulary** Read the words in the list. They are words from the next reading. Listen to their pronunciation. Do not look them up in a dictionary. Check (✓) the words that you don't know.

Nouns		Verbs	Adjectives
▨ body language	▨ genders	▨ communicate	▨ comfortable
▨ equality	▨ hierarchy	▨ connect	▨ equal
▨ eye contact	▨ position	▨ nod	▨ funny
▨ fields	▨ suggestions		▨ similar

Strategy

Understanding New Words in a Reading

You do not always need to use a dictionary to find the meaning of a new word. Sometimes the meaning is in the sentence before or after the word.

Example

Men and women also have different body language. They have different ways to communicate with their face and body.

(*Body language* means different ways to communicate with the face and body.)

Sometimes the meaning is after the phrase *in other words*.

Example

Experts are paying attention to the differences in the ways businesswomen and men think and communicate—in other words, talk with and understand other people.

(*Communicate* means to talk with and understand other people.)

4 **Understanding New Words in a Reading** The meanings of these words are in the next article. Find the words and underline their meanings.

connect	equality	eye contact	genders	hierarchy	nod

Read

 5 **Reading an Article** Read the following article. Don't use your dictionary. If you don't know some words, try to figure out their meaning. Then do the activities.

Men and Women in Business

A   In some **fields**, such as engineering, there are more men than women. In other fields, there are more women than men—in education, for example. But in business, the numbers of men and women are almost the same. Perhaps for this reason, experts are paying attention to the differences in the ways businesswomen and men think and **communicate**—in other words, 5 talk with and understand other people. The two **genders**—women and men—might work in the same place and do the same job, but they live in different worlds of work.

What's Important, and How Do People Communicate It?

B   What is important when people work in a group? The two genders often have different ideas about this. For women, **equality** is important; 10

in other words, women usually want all people in a group to have the same **position**. They often see conversation as a way to **connect** with other 15 people—in other words, to be close to them and find ways that they are **similar**—almost the same. For men, it's important to have a high position in the 20 **hierarchy** (the system from low to high positions). They usually see conversation as a way to give and get information but also a way to climb up in the hierarchy. 25 For example, a man might have a high position if he has more information than others or can tell **funny** stories.

Body Language

C   Men and women also have different **body language**. They have different ways to communicate with their face and body. Imagine an office full of people of both genders. Notice their body language. Women like eye contact. They need to look directly into each other's eyes. Men usually don't like **eye contact**. In a meeting, women like to sit face to face. Men like to sit side by side. In conversation, people of both genders often **nod**—move their head up and down. This means "Yes," but there are other meanings. For women, it usually means, "I'm listening to you. I understand." But for men, it usually means, "I agree." As you see, the two genders often communicate in different ways with their faces and bodies.

30

35

How People Solve Problems

D   What happens when there are problems in the workplace? Men and women have different ways to solve the problems. Women, who feel **comfortable** with equality, want to talk about the problem and solve it together with other people. Men want to find answers and end the problem quickly. A woman who needs help usually asks for help. This is easy for her. It's a small connection with another person. A man doesn't like to ask for help. He thinks it puts him in a low position in the hierarchy. But a man likes to *give* help because this moves him up in the hierarchy.

40

45

Conclusion

E   You might ask, "Who's right—the men or the women?" Experts usually agree: there is no "right" or "wrong." The two styles of working are just different. Most experts have these **suggestions**: people in business need to understand differences between men's and women's styles. But also, each gender sometimes needs to try the style of the other gender!

50

6 **Identifying the Main Ideas and Details** Read the sentences below. Check (✓) *Men* or *Women* for each sentence. You can find the information in the reading.

	Men	Women
The field of engineering has more _____.	✓	
The field of education has more _____.	✗	✓
Equality is important to them.		✓
They see conversation as a way to connect with others.		✓
It's important to them to have a high position.	✓	
They sit side by side.	✓	
They sit face to face and like eye contact.		✓
They often nod to mean "I'm listening to you."		✓
They often nod to mean "I agree."	✓	

7 **Checking Vocabulary** Write the words for the meanings below. For help, look back at the boldfaced words in paragraphs A, B, C, and E of the reading.

Meaning	Word
almost the same *(not equality)*	Similar
making people laugh	funny
men and women	genders
looking directly into other people's eyes	eye contact
ideas about what to do	suggestions
move the head up and down	nod
the system from low to high	hierarchy

8 **Identifying a Good Summary** Read the summaries below. Which is a good summary of the article "Men and Women in Business"? Why is it good? Why are the others not good? Choose the best one. Compare your answer with a partner's.

details

A. Men and women have different ideas about what is important in a group. Women like equality. In other words, they want everyone in a group to have the same position. Men think it's important to have a high position in the hierarchy. The two genders also use conversation differently in groups.

details

B. The two genders—men and women—are very different. For example, their body language is different. Women usually sit face to face and have eye contact. Men often sit side by side and do not have eye contact. Also, when they nod, the meaning is often different for women and men.

C. Men and women in business think and communicate differently. They have different ideas about hierarchy. Their body language and ways of solving problems are also different. Experts tell us that there is no "right" or "wrong"— just "different."

9 Discussing the Reading Talk about your answers to the following questions.

1. In your experience, is position in the hierarchy of a group more important to men than to women? Give an example.

2. Would you like to have a high position in a group, or would you like to be in a group where everyone's position is equal? Why?

3. What do *you* mean when you nod? List all of the meanings for you.

4. The reading is about men and women in *business*. In what other situations can you find differences between men and women (or boys and girls)?

5. The reading is about how men and women communicate in business in the United States. How is the situation in your country similar and/or different?

PART 2 Main Ideas and Details

Gender and Communication on Campus

Before You Read

1 Making Predictions Look at the pictures. How are they different? What are the girls doing? What are the boys doing?

2 Previewing Vocabulary Read the words in the list. They are words from the next reading. Listen to their pronunciation. Do not look them up in a dictionary. Check (✓) the words that you don't know.

Nouns	Verbs	Adjectives
▣ participation	▣ argue	▣ active
▣ status	▣ participate	▣ personal

3 Reading Background Information Read these paragraphs about where gender differences begin.

Gender and Communication on Campus

A   Experts on education find that boys and girls, men and women, usually do better in single-gender classes. In other words, they do well in a class with other students of the same gender. Why? Their learning styles are different. The two genders feel comfortable with different styles of teaching.

B   As children, boys usually play in big groups with a hierarchy. They often 5 **argue** about rules to their games. They are often loud and very **active**. As children, girls usually sit and talk with one best friend or in a small group. They often talk about their feelings or tell **personal** stories about their lives. In school, boys do well in a loud, active class. Girls do well in a class that has small groups. Interestingly, experts tell us that girls have better hearing than 10 boys. In a classroom, it sometimes seems that boys aren't paying attention. Often, this is because they don't *hear* a teacher with a quiet voice.

C   In many college classes in the United States, **participation** is important. Teachers expect students to speak in class. In discussions, students often argue different sides of an issue. Men usually feel comfortable with this 15 style of teaching. Speaking in a large group seems natural to them. It gives them **status**—a higher position—in the hierarchy of the class. Women don't usually feel comfortable with this style. Many women don't **participate** much in class discussions, but they do participate when the class breaks into small groups. 20

After You Read

4 Identifying the Main Idea What is the main idea of the reading?

(A) Girls usually feel comfortable in small groups; boys feel comfortable in large ones.

(B) Men usually participate more in college classes than women do.

(C) The two genders play differently as children and have different learning styles.

5 Identifying Details Read the article again. Then answer the two questions below. You may check (✓) more than one answer for each question.

1. What does the reading say about females (girls and women)? Check all that apply.

   a. _✓_ Girls often talk with one best friend or in a small group.

   b. _____ Girls often argue about rules to their games.

   c. _✓_ Girls have better hearing than boys do.

   d. _✓_ Girls and women don't usually feel comfortable speaking in a large class.

2. What does the reading say about males (boys and men)? Check all that apply.

   a. _✓_ Boys play in big groups with a hierarchy.

   b. _✓_ Boys do well in a loud, active class.

   c. _____ Males usually don't feel comfortable when they need to argue different sides of an issue.

   d. _✓_ Speaking in class gives men status in the hierarchy of the class.

Strategy

Recognizing Conclusions

A *conclusion* is the end of an article. It is similar to a summary. (See page 30.) A good conclusion has the main information of the article, but it doesn't have small details. Also, it doesn't leave out *important* information. A conclusion often begins with or includes one of these phrases:

- In conclusion,…
- Clearly,…
- As we see,…

Summary — includes main info
Con - focuses on results or outcomes
Generally short + concise

6 Identifying a Good Conclusion Read the conclusions below. Which is a good conclusion for the article "Gender and Communication on Campus"? Why is it good? Why are the others not good? Choose the best one. Compare your answer with a partner's.

A. As we see, boys play in large, loud groups. They often argue about the rules to their games. For this reason, boys do well in a loud, active class. Then, in college, men feel comfortable in a class discussion when they need to argue one side of an issue.

B. Boys and girls have different ways of playing. In school—and later, in college—the two genders also have different styles of learning. Clearly, teachers need to understand this and use teaching styles to help both genders do well.

C. In conclusion, girls often play with just one friend or in a small group. In school—and later, in college—they usually participate more in classes that have discussions in small groups, not the whole class.

Strategy

college studi. in the U.S

Reading Faster

Students usually need to read fast because they have to read many books each year. Also, they can understand more if they read fast. One way to read faster is to read silently—not out loud.

Another way to read faster is to read groups of words, or phrases, not one word at a time. Look at the example. Then do the activity.

Example

Slow │ readers │ read │ one │ word │ at │ a │ time, │ like │ this.

Fast readers │ usually read │ words in phrases, │ like this. │ Of course, │ this helps them │ to read faster, │ but it also │ helps them │ to understand more.

7 **Practice: Reading in Phrases** Read the following sentences in phrases. Read silently; in other words, do not speak.

Males and females │ sometimes seem │ to speak different languages.
They think differently. │ Their body language │ is different, too.
For example, imagine a man and woman │ in conversation. │ The man is speaking.
The woman is nodding. │ She is thinking, │ "I'm listening. │ I understand."
He thinks she means │ "I agree." │ Maybe they need │ to go to language class:
Gender as a Second Language!

Now read the paragraph. Focus on the phrases, not the separate words:

Read silently\read aloud

Men and women sometimes seem to speak different languages. They like to talk about different things. They also have different ideas about what is important. Sometimes they don't listen to each other. A woman makes a suggestion, but her husband doesn't really listen. A man tries to help with a problem, but his wife doesn't like it. Maybe they should go to language school!

8 Discussing the Reading With a group, fill in the chart. Then talk about the questions that follow.

On the chart, write differences between males' and females' ways of communicating (from the readings on pages 80–81 and 84). How many can you find?

Males	Females
· as children, are active and loud	· as children, often sit and talk
· play in a big group	*want equality*
like high pos	*lk conversat.; mk eye contact*
sit side by side	*sit face-to-face*
find answers\solutions quickly	*talk abt problems + sol*
argue, give help	*ask for help*
poorer hearing	*talk abt. feelings*
lk to speak in ly grps	*discuss in small groups*

1. How was your experience as a child similar to or different from the readings?

2. How is your experience as a student, now, similar to or different from the readings?

3. Do you agree or disagree with most of the readings? Why?

9 Writing in Your Journal Choose one topic below. Write about it for five minutes. Use some of the vocabulary that you have learned in this chapter.

- something that you learned about how men and women think
- body language such as nodding and eye contact
- your ideas about working in a group; do you like equality or hierarchy?
- how you and your classmates are different from, or similar to, the students in Paragraph C on page 84.
- ways the students are communicating in the photo below

Using Inclusive Language

FOCUS

Understanding Language and Sexism

Sexism is the belief that one gender (male or female) is better than the other gender. Many people believe that language can be *sexist*; that is, language can give us the idea that men are better or more important than women. Some common phrases in English traditionally name men first; for example, *men and women*, *husbands and wives*, and *Mr. and Mrs.*

There used to be words for jobs that included the idea of only men doing these jobs—words such as *fireman* and *mailman.* Some people believe these words give us the idea that only men can fight fires or deliver the mail. Therefore, most people now use the words *fire fighter* and *mail carrier* to include the idea of both men and women. To make language more *gender neutral* or equal, people are changing the way they use langauge.

1 **Matching Words** Read the words below. Match the words in Column A with the gender-neutral words in Column B.

Column A (only male or female)

1. __f__ man-made
2. __h__ mankind
3. __d__ policeman
4. __a__ chairman
5. __i__ actress
6. __c__ wife or husband
7. __j__ housewife
8. __b__ salesman
9. __g__ waiter/waitress
10. __e__ stewardess
11. __l__ headmaster
12. __k__ manpower

Column B (either male or female)

a. chair or chairperson
b. salesperson
c. spouse
d. police officer
e. flight attendant
f. not natural, made by humans
g. server (in a restaurant)
h. humanity, people, human beings
i. actor
j. homemaker
k. staff, workers
l. principal, director

Using Gender-Neutral Possessive Adjectives

Possessive adjectives show gender; *his* is used for a male, *her* is used for a female. But sometimes we don't know if a noun is male or female, or the noun may include both genders. In such cases, you can use *his or her.* Another style is to make the noun plural and use the possessive adjective *their,* which can be male or female or include both.

Every student needs **his** laptop.

(*His* refers to a male. We can use this only when every student is a male.)

Every student needs **his or her** laptop.

(Using *his or her* includes both male and female students.)

Students need **their** laptops.

(Making the sentence plural includes both male and female students.)

[handwritten margin note: What if you don't know if a word is only men or only women? What can you do?]

---

2 **Using Possessive Adjectives** Read the sentences below. Write *his, her,* or *his or her* in the blanks. Then rewrite sentences 4, 7 and 9 by changing the subject, verb and object if necessary and by using the pronoun *their.*

1. A good student never uses ___his or her___ cell phone in class.

   _____Good students never use their cell phones in class._____

2. The tall man left ___his___ laptop on the table.

3. The woman was angry at ___her___ husband.

4. A doctor will pay a lot of money for ___his or her___ education.

   ___Doctors pay a lot of $ for their educ.___

5. Some police officer parked ___his or her___ car on the street in front of my house.

6. My teacher, Ms. Smith, always answers ___her___ e-mail from us.

7. Every teacher needs to know ___his or her___ subject well.

   ___Teachers need to know their subjects well.___

8. Mr. Jones is my Information Technology 101 professor, and I love ___his___ class.

9. Every person can make ___his or her___ own decision.

   ___People can make their own decision(s).___

10. A man can change ___his or her___ mind, and a woman can change _____ mind, too.

1 **Reviewing Vocabulary** Read each sentence below and write True or False. New words from this chapter are underlined.

1. When you <u>nod</u>, you move your hands. _____False_____

2. Coffee and tea are <u>similar</u>. _____true_____

3. Animals that live in groups may have a <u>hierarchy</u>. _____+_____

4. If I have ten dollars and Fred has ten dollars, we have an <u>equal</u> amount of money. _____+_____

5. Medicine, teaching, and going to the movies are all <u>fields</u>. _____f_____
   engineering

6. Some movies are <u>funny</u>, and some movies aren't. _____+_____

7. Women and men are the <u>same</u> <u>gender</u>. _____f_____
   dy

8. The president of a company has a <u>low</u> <u>status</u>. _____f_____
   high

9. If you <u>connect</u> with someone, you probably ~~don't~~ want to visit him or her. _____f_____

10. A <u>spouse</u> usually lives with you. _____+_____

Now rewrite the false sentences to make them true.

Example: *When you nod, you move your head.*

_____

2 **Listening: Focusing on High-Frequency Words.** Listen and fill in the blanks in the sentences. Some of the words are new and some of the words are not new.

Men and women also have different ___body___ language. They have different ways to ___comm___ with their face and body. Imagine an office full of ___ppl___ of both genders. Notice their body language. Women like eye ___contact___. They need to look directly into each ___other's___ eyes. Men usually don't   5 like eye ___contact___. In a meeting, women like to sit face to face. Men like to sit side by ___sde___. In conversation, people of both ___genders___ often nod—move their head up and down.

This means "Yes," but there are other meanings. For women, it usually __means__ , "I'm listening to you. I understand." But for men, it   10 usually means, "I __agree__." As you see, the two genders often communicate in different ways with their faces and bodies.

3 **Completing Sentences** Read the words in the box and then read the sentences below. Write the correct word from the box in each of the blanks. Remember to read the whole sentence before you answer. These vocabulary words are from Chapters 1 to 5.

advice	experts	online	population	public
argue	garage	percent	prediction	quit
chronic	heart	personal	profit	stress
computers	information			

1. Five years ago __computers__ and smart phones were many times slower than they are today.

2. Jeff Bezos __quit__ his good job. He then started Amazon.com in a __garage__ at his parents' house.

3. Many doctors believe that __stress__, especially __chronic__ stress that you have all the time, can be very bad for your whole body, especially your __heart__.

4. There is a lot of __information__ on the Internet, but you have to be careful because sometimes the __advice__ you find there can be wrong or dangerous.

5. One Internet business had an increase in __profit__ of 300 __percent__ in one year.

6. Most couples do not like to __argue__ in __public__. They prefer to fight at home.

7. One __prediction__ of scientists and other __experts__ is that the __population__ of the world will become smaller and smaller in the future.

8. You have to be careful how much __personal__ information you put __online__.

Building Vocabulary Complete the crossword puzzle with words from the box. These words are from Chapter 5.

active	equal	genders	participate
argue	feelings	hierarchy	position
communicate	fields	imagine	similar
discussion	funny	nod	solve

Across

2. join in an activity
4. for example, happiness, or sadness
6. think inside your head
9. move your head up and down
11. a system of high and low status
12. fix a problem
15. the same
16. for example, first or second
17. disagree in a conversation

Down

1. kinds of work or study
3. talk and listen
5. men or women
7. a talk about something
10. not exactly the same but…
13. moving around a lot
14. something that makes you laugh is

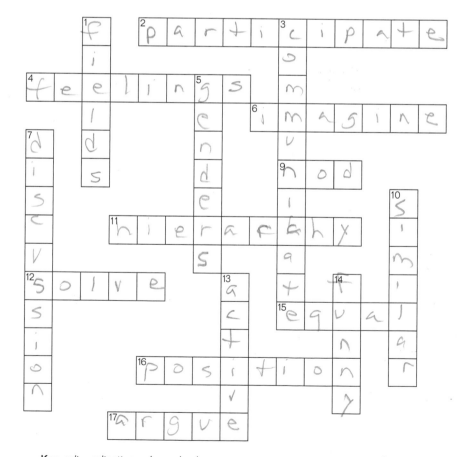

Key: *adj.* = adjective; *adv.* = adverb; *n.* = noun; *prep.* = preposition; *v.* = verb

Self-Assessment Log

Read the lists below. Check (✓) the strategies and vocabulary that you learned in this chapter. Look through the chapter or ask your instructor about the strategies and words that you do not understand.

Reading and Vocabulary-Building Strategies

☐ Understanding a graph
☐ Understanding new words in a reading
☐ Recognizing conclusions
☐ Reading faster
☐ Understanding and using gender-neutral language
☐ Focusing on high-frequency words

Target Vocabulary

Nouns	Verbs	Adjectives
body* language*	argue	active
equality	communicate	comfortable
eye* contact	connect	equal*
fields*	nod	funny
genders	participate	personal
hierarchy		similar*
participation		
position*		
status		
suggestions		

* These words are among the 1,000 most frequently used words in English.

Sleep and Dreams

"Dreams say what they
mean, but they don't
say it in daytime
language."

Gail Godwin
American writer

In this **CHAPTER**

In Part 1, you will read about some theories and research on sleep and dreams. In the rest of this chapter, you will read about, explore, and discuss the art, science, and stories of dreams.

Connecting to the Topic

1 What do you see in the photo? What is the woman doing? What is the man doing?

2 What are some sleep problems that people have? Name five.

3 What are four questions that the researcher (the woman in the white coat) might have about sleep and dreams? Discuss them.

The Purpose of Sleep and Dreams

Before You Read

1 **Interviewing Students** Look at the questions in the chart below. Decide on your answers. Then walk around the room and ask four students the questions. Put their answers in this chart.

Questions	Student 1	Student 2	Student 3	Student 4
1. How many hours of sleep do you need each night?				
2. Why do we sleep?				
3. Does everyone dream?				
4. What do you think a road in a dream means?				

▲ Do babies dream?

2 **Previewing Vocabulary** Read the words below. Listen to their pronunciation. Do not look them up in a dictionary. Put a check mark (✓) next to the words that you don't know.

Nouns
- childhood
- desires
- emotions
- evidence
- Freud
- hormone
- logic
- psychologists
- purpose
- research
- stage
- symbols
- theories (theory)
- vision

Verbs
- occurs
- predict
- repair
- wonder

Adjective
- awake

Adverb
- however

3 **Understanding New Words** In Chapters 1–5, you learned ways to understand new words in a reading. Below are some new words from the next reading. Try to understand their meanings from these sentences, without a dictionary. Write the meanings on the lines.

1. Many people <u>wonder</u>: Why do we sleep? Why do we dream? They ask themselves about the reasons for sleep and dreams.

   wonder = <u>*ask themselves*</u>

2. There was a lot of <u>evidence</u> that George killed Mr. Smith. Police found George's gun in Mr. Smith's house. Also, two people saw George leaving Mr. Smith's house. In addition, everyone knew that George hated Mr. Smith.

   evidence = <u>*proof that smthg is true*</u>

3. Our bodies produce more of a <u>growth hormone</u> (a chemical that helps us grow) while we sleep.

   hormone = <u>*a chem. in the body*</u>

4. A <u>psychologist</u> studies people's behavior. Some psychologists, such as Sigmund Freud, have strong beliefs about dreams.

   psychologist = <u>*a person who studies ppl's behav.*</u>

5. Can dreams tell us something about our <u>emotions</u>—our feelings?

   emotions = <u>*feelings*</u>

6. Maybe these are <u>symbols</u>. In other words, they mean *other* things. For example, a road in a dream might be a symbol of the direction of a dreamer's life.

   symbols = <u>*things that mean other things*</u>

7. When we are <u>awake</u>, we don't dream. We dream only when we're asleep.

   awake = <u>*not asleep*</u>

8. Those parts of the brain are for <u>vision</u> (the ability to see), and <u>logic</u> (the ability to think and understand).

   vision = <u>*the ability to see*</u>

   logic = <u>*" ability to thk + understand*</u>

Strategy

Finding the Meaning of New Words: Meaning After _Or_

You do not always need to use a dictionary to find the meaning of a new word. The meaning of a new word is sometimes after the word _or_ in a sentence.

Example

> There are many **theories**, or opinions.
> (_Theories_ means "opinions.")

4 **Finding the Meaning of New Words** The meanings of these words are in the next article. Find the words and circle their meanings.

desires	occurs	purpose	repair	research	stage

Read

5 **Reading an Article** Read the following article. Don't use your dictionary. If you don't know some words, try to figure out their meanings. Then do the activities.

The Purpose of Sleep and Dreams

A Many people **wonder**: Why do we sleep? Why do we dream? They ask themselves the **purpose**, or reason. There are many **theories**, or opinions, about this, but scientists don't know if these ideas are correct.

Theories of Sleep

B One theory of sleep says that during the day, we use many important chemicals in our bodies and brains. We need sleep to make new chemicals and **repair**, or fix, our bodies. This theory is called the "Repair Theory." One piece of **evidence** for this theory is that our bodies produce more of a **growth hormone** (a chemical that helps us grow) while we sleep. Another theory is that the purpose of sleep is to dream. Dreaming **occurs**, or happens, only during one **stage**, or period, of sleep—REM (Rapid Eye Movement) sleep. REM sleep occurs about every 90 minutes and lasts for about 20 minutes. Some scientists believe that REM sleep helps us to remember things, but other scientists don't agree.

5

10

Dream Theories

C   Whatever the reason for sleep, everyone sleeps, and everyone dreams every night. Many times we don't remember our dreams, but we still dream. Like sleep, no one knows exactly why we dream or what dreams mean. There have been many theories about dreams throughout history. Many cultures believe that dreams can **predict** the future—that they can tell us what is going to happen to us. **However**, some people believe that dreams are only a form of entertainment.

D   **Psychologists** such as Sigmund **Freud** say that dreams are not predictions of the future. Psychologists have strong beliefs about dreams. However, these scientists don't always agree with each other. There are several different theories about the purpose of dreaming.

E   Freud, who wrote around the year 1900, said that dreams can tell us about our **emotions**—feelings—and **desires**, or wishes. Freud believed that our dreams are full of **symbols**. In other words, things in our dreams mean *other* things. For example, a road in a dream isn't really a road. It might be a symbol of the dreamer's life. Freud thought that dreams are about things from our past, from our **childhood**. Other psychologists say no.

▲ Dreams occur only during REM sleep.

They believe that dreams are about the *present*, about our ideas, desires, and problems *now*. Other psychologists say that dreams have no meaning at all.

New Evidence

F   We still don't know why we dream. However, there is interesting new evidence from **research**, or studies, about the brain. When we are **awake**, many parts of our brain are active, for example the parts for emotions, **vision** (the ability to see), **logic** (the ability to think and understand), and others. However, when we are asleep and dreaming, the part of the brain for *logic* is not active. Maybe this new evidence answers one common question: Why do dreams seem so crazy?

After You Read

6 Finding Details What are some theories about sleep and dreams? Look back at the reading. Find information and fill in the chart.

Theories	
Why do we sleep?	1. To repair our bodies
	2. to dream
Why do we dream?	1. dreams may predict the fut.
	2. a form of entertainment
	3. Freud said: Dreams tell abt emotions
	4. " " " present problems
	5. " he no meaning at all

7 Working with New Words Write the vocabulary words for the meanings below. For help, look back at the boldfaced words in the reading. (Look before the word *or.*)

Meaning	Vocabulary Word
1. reason	purpose
2. opinions	theories
3. fix	repair
4. happens	occurs
5. period of time	stage
6. wishes	desires
7. studies	research

Strategy

Understanding Words from Their Parts

The beginning or ending of some words can help you with their meanings. Here are four:

Board *(handwritten)*

Word Part and Meaning	Example
• *un-* can mean "not"	**un**happy
• *-er* can mean "a person who"	writ**er**
• *-ist* can mean "a person's job"	scient**ist**
• *-hood* can mean "the situation or stage of life when a person…"	parent**hood** adult**hood**

(handwritten notes in right margin):
If you're not happy, you are ___
If you write, you are a ___
The stage of life when you are a parent is called ___

8 **Understanding Words from Their Parts** Write a word for each definition below. Use a word in the definition and a part from the Strategy Box above: *un-, -er, -ist, -hood.*

1. not interesting = _uninteresting_
2. a person who dreams = _dreamer_
3. the stage of life when a person is a child = _childhood_
4. a person who is in the profession/job of psychology
   = _psychologist_
5. not comfortable = _uncomf._
6. a person who does research = _researcher_
7. a person who teaches = _teacher_

9 **Discussing the Reading** Discuss your answers to the following questions.

1. Do you remember your dreams? What do you think dreams mean?
2. What does your family or culture think about dreams?
3. With your group, summarize the theories about why we dream. Look at the reading for help.
4. Do you believe one of the theories from Activity 6 about why we dream? Why or why not?

A Dream Narrative

Before You Read

1 **Thinking About the Topic** For each question, choose the answer that is correct for you. Then share and discuss your answers with a group.

1. How often do you remember your dreams?
   - (A) every night
   - (B) often (four or five times a week)
   - (C) sometimes (once or twice a week)
   - (D) rarely (once a month)
   - (E) never

2. How often do you have nightmares (dreams that are scary or frightening)?
   - (A) every night
   - (B) often (four or five times a week)
   - (C) sometimes (once or twice a week)
   - (D) rarely (once a month)
   - (E) never

3. How often do you talk about your dreams with friends or relatives?
   - (A) every time I dream
   - (B) often
   - (C) sometimes
   - (D) rarely
   - (E) never

4. How often do you try to interpret your dreams—in other words, try to figure out their meaning?
   - (A) every time I dream
   - (B) often
   - (C) sometimes
   - (D) rarely
   - (E) never

2 Previewing Vocabulary Read the words below. Listen to their pronunciation. Do not look them up in a dictionary. Put a check mark (✓) next to the words that you don't know.

Verbs	**Adjectives**	**Adverb**	**Expression**
▧ realized	▧ anxious	▧ outside	▧ make sense
▧ traveling	▧ complicated		
	▧ familiar		
	▧ unfamiliar		

Strategy

Finding the Meaning of New Words in Context
Sometimes the meaning of a word can be found in the sentence or phrase that follows the new word.

Example
We had our lunch **outside**. It was a warm day, and we sat under a tree.
(*outside* = not on the inside of something; not in a building)

3 Finding the Meaning of New Words in Context Find the meaning of the underlined words. Look in the sentence or phrase that follows them. Choose the best answer.

1. My friends like to <u>travel</u>. Last week they went to Hong Kong. I prefer to stay here in my own city on my vacation.

   (A) study   (B) go places   (C) exercise

2. I was very <u>anxious</u>. This always happens to me. I'm always very worried before an exam.

   (A) happy   (B) busy   (C) nervous

3. I was in a new city. Everything was strange. Nothing was <u>familiar</u>.

   (A) from my family   (B) something that I knew   (C) beautiful

4. The math problem was very <u>complicated</u>. I couldn't do it, and my teacher couldn't do it either.

   (A) easy   (B) interesting   (C) difficult

5. You can't stay home today! Don't you <u>realize</u> that we have a really important exam?

   (A) understand   (B) want   (C) wonder

6. The story <u>didn't make sense</u>. I read it four times, and I still didn't understand it.

   (A) was easy to understand   (B) was interesting   (C) was without logic

4 Reading a Narrative Read this narrative (story). Then answer the questions.

A Dream Narrative

This is the dream of a 40-year-old businessman. He is married and has two children. He goes to a psychologist because he feels **anxious** a lot. The psychologist told him to write down his dreams. This is his dream from June 7.

Dream 6/7: In my dream I was in a large city. It was very big and very dark. The city seemed like New York, but it didn't look like the real New York. I was in a friend's apartment. It was comfortable. After a few minutes, I left and went out on the street, alone. I walked for a while. Then I realized I was lost. I couldn't find my friend's apartment again. I started to feel uncomfortable. I tried to return to the apartment, but all of the streets looked unfamiliar and completely different, and I didn't know my friend's address. I began to feel anxious.

I kept walking. I wanted to find something familiar. It was getting late. I decided to go home. I knew my home was outside the city. I saw buses on the street, but I didn't know which one to take. I couldn't find a way to leave the city. There was a way to get home, but I didn't know it. I asked for directions. The people answered, but they didn't make any sense. All their directions were very complicated, and I couldn't understand them.

Suddenly I was on a boat. The boat was traveling across a very dangerous river. It was dark. The river was very dirty. There was garbage in it. I couldn't see the other side of the river, and I was afraid. I began to think, "I'll never get home." I tried to ask for help, but no one listened to me. Then I woke up.

▲ A dream

5 Identifying the Main Idea What is the main idea of the reading?

    Ⓐ A businessman was in a big city at night.

→ Ⓑ A man wrote about his dream for his psychologist.

    Ⓒ In a dream, a man was trying to go home, but it was difficult.

6 Finding Details Read the dream narrative again. Then read the details below. Put checks (✓) next to the details that are in the narrative.

_____✓_____ The man was anxious.

_____✓_____ A psychologist tried to help him.

_____ He walked to his psychologist's office in the city.

_____✓_____ In his dream, he was in a big city.

_____ It was morning in his dream.

_____✓_____ In the dream, he wanted to go home.

_____✓_____ In the dream, he had problems on his way home.

7 Understanding Pronouns Find the meaning of each underlined pronoun. Highlight it. Then draw an arrow from the pronoun to its meaning.

1. The city seemed like New York, but <u>it</u> didn't look like the real New York.
2. I was in <u>a friend's apartment</u>. <u>It</u> was comfortable.
3. On the street I saw <u>buses</u>, but I didn't know which <u>one</u> to take.
4. There was <u>a way to get home</u>, but I didn't know <u>it</u>.
5. All <u>their directions</u> were very complicated, and I couldn't understand <u>them</u>.

FOCUS

Understanding Mood

The *mood* of a piece of writing is the "feeling," or emotion in it. One way to understand the mood is to notice the adjectives. For example, a writer might use the adjectives *happy, wonderful,* and *beautiful* for a positive mood or *anxious, unhappy,* and *horrible* for a negative mood.

8 Understanding Mood Find all of the adjectives in the dream narrative. Highlight them. In your opinion, what is the mood of this dream? Discuss your opinions with a partner.

9 Discussing the Reading Look back at Paragraph E on page 99. Then discuss your answers to the following questions with a group.

1. What might psychologists say about the man's dream on page 104? What are his emotions?
2. What might be some symbols in his dream? In your opinion, what might they mean?

10 Writing in Your Journal Choose one topic below. Write about it for five minutes. Use some of the vocabulary that you have learned in this chapter.

- something that you learned about sleep or dreams
- a dream that you have had
- your opinion of dreams

PART 3 Practical English

Searching the Web

Using the Internet

Searching for Information on the Internet

Searching the Web can be difficult in a foreign language. Some websites are useful and some are not useful. When you do a search, look at the search results page. You need to scan the information—read very quickly and get a general idea of each website. Then decide if it is useful to you.

Example

Below is an example of a search results page on the Internet. Note the meaning of the following terms at the end of the website name:

.com = commercial (indicates a business)

.org = organization (an organization, not usually a business)

.edu = education (indicates a college or university)

| dreams | **Submit** |

Search Results

1 • Amazon.com: Akira Kurosawa's Dreams (1990): DVD
   Short films by the famous Japanese director... www.amazon.com

2 • What Dreams Are Made Of - Newsweek Health - MSNBC.com
   Article on the study and history of dreams, Newsweek Magazine...
   www.msnbc.msn.com

3 • Dreams Bed Superstore
   Dreams is Britain's leading bed seller, selling a wide range of beds. Sells all types
   and kinds of beds... www.dreamsplc.com

4 • Dreams: FAQ

This site will answer most of your general questions about dreams.... people who did that research in the 1950s and...

http://www2.ucsc.edu/dreams/FAQ/ International Conference

5 • The DREAMS Foundation

(Dream Research and Experimental Approaches to the Mechanisms of Sleep) This dream blog is pretty amazing... bloggers across the Internet have written down their dreams.... http://dreams.ca

6 • Dreams and Wishes Quotes

Quotes and quotations from the website Famous Quotes... All our dreams can come true, if we have the courage to pursue them. Walt Disney

http://www.goodquotes.com/quote/walt-disney/all-our-dreams-can-come-true-if-we-hav

1 **Searching for Information on the Internet** You are in a college freshman psychology course. You have to do a four-page research paper about dreams. Match each website description below to a website in the Strategy Box on page 106 and 107. Write the number of the site on the line.

a. __2__ This site has an article from a popular news magazine. It is probably a good place for basic information about the subject.

b. __4__ The Web address of this site has "ucsc.edu". The "edu" tells us it is probably a university. It answers "frequently asked questions" (FAQ).

c. __1__ This website sells books and movies. This site is on the list because the title of the movie is *Dreams*.

d. __5__ On this website, people can describe their dreams and share them with other people.

e. __6__ This is a site with quotes about different subjects. This page gives us quotes about dreams.

f. __3__ This site sells beds.

What are the three best sites for your research paper? Why? Write your choices and explanations below.

2

4

5

2 **Choosing Words for an Online Search** Using more than one word in your search can help you find good sites. <u>Look at the words in the box and circle</u> or <u>highlight the words that you think would help in the search in Activity 1.</u>

baseball	Freud	research	theories
dreams	humans	sleep	university
freshman	paper	student	wake

Imagine you are writing a paper about new theories on the reason people sleep. Write four words that you might use to search for information on the Internet. Choose words from the box above or think of other words. Share your answers with classmates. What are the best four words?

_____   _____

_____   _____

PART 4 Vocabulary Practice

1 **Reviewing Vocabulary: True/False** Read each sentence below. Check (✓) *True* or *False*. Vocabulary words from this and previous chapters are underlined.

	True	False
1. <u>Emotions</u> and feelings are almost the same.	☑	☐
2. If you're <u>awake</u>, you're not asleep.	☑	☐
3. If you use <u>logic</u>, you make decisions with your emotions.	☐	☑
4. An <u>anxious</u> person is not usually nervous.	☐	☑
5. <u>Childhood</u> is one <u>stage</u> in human life.	☑	☐
6. Most movies and stories have a <u>narrative</u>.	☑	☐
7. If you understand the class, it doesn't <u>make sense</u>.	☐	☑
8. If you have a <u>theory</u>, you should have some <u>evidence</u> for that theory.	☑	☐

2 **Listening: Focusing on High-Frequency Words** Listen and write the missing words in the blanks on the next page. If you don't know, then guess.

Freud, who wrote around the year 1900, said that dreams can tell us about our emotions—feelings—and ___desires___, or wishes. Freud ___believed___ that our dreams are full of symbols. In other words, things in our dreams mean *other* things. For example, a road in a ___dream___ isn't really a road. It might be a ___symbol___ of the dreamer's life. Freud ___thought___ that dreams are about things from our past, from our ___childhood___. Other psychologists say no. They ___believe___ that dreams are about the *present*, about our ideas, desires, and problems *now*. ___Other___ psychologists say that dreams have no meaning at all.

3 Using Your Vocabulary Use these words from Chapter 6 to make your own sentences.

1. stage / dreaming / occurs

   Dreaming occurs during the REM sleep stage.

2. purpose / sleep / scientists

   _____

3. cultures / predict / dreams

   _____

4. dreams / psychologists / research

   _____

5. childhood / I / often

   _____

4 Building Vocabulary Complete the crossword puzzle. These words are from Chapters 3, 5, and 6.

argue	desires	predict	stage
average	evidence	purpose	theory
awake	Freud	repair	traditional
boss	logic	research	unfamiliar
childhood	nod	similar	wedding

Across

1. opposite of *familiar* (adj.)
5. an idea a scientist has about something (n.)
9. almost the same (adj.)
10. see ahead into the future (v.)
11. disagree with words (v.)
12. wishes, wants (n.)
15. someone important at work (n.)
16. opposite of *asleep* (adj.)
17. a famous psychologist (n.)
18. the method you use when you think carefully (n.)
19. proof that something is true (n.)

Down

2. scientific study (n.)
3. life from birth to about age 13 (n.)
4. move your head up and down to say "yes" (v.)
6. like customs in a culture (adj.)
7. Childhood is the first _____ of life. (n.)
8. fix; make something good again (v.)
11. The _____ of 3 and 9 is 6. (n.)
13. the reason for an action or a thing (n.)
14. a ceremony when people get married (n.)

Key: *adj.* = adjective; *adv.* = adverb; *n.* = noun; *prep.* = preposition; *v.* = verb

Self-Assessment Log

Read the lists below. Check (✓) the strategies and vocabulary that you learned in this chapter. Look through the chapter or ask your instructor about the strategies and words that you do not understand.

Reading and Vocabulary-Building Strategies

☐ Finding the meaning of new words: meaning after *or*
☐ Finding details
☐ Understanding words from their parts
☐ Finding the meaning of new words in context
☐ Identifying the main idea
☐ Understanding pronouns
☐ Understanding mood
☐ Searching for information on the Internet

Target Vocabulary

Nouns	Verbs	Adjectives	Adverbs
▨ childhood	▨ occurs	▨ anxious	▨ however*
▨ desires	▨ predict	▨ awake	▨ outside*
▨ emotions	▨ realized	▨ complicated	
▨ evidence	▨ repair	▨ familiar	**Expression**
▨ Freud	▨ traveling	▨ unfamiliar	▨ make* sense*
▨ hormone	(travel)*		
▨ logic	▨ wonder*		
▨ psychologists			
▨ purpose			
▨ research			
▨ stage			
▨ symbols*			
▨ theories			
(theory)			
▨ vision			

*These words are among the 1,000 most-frequently used words in English.

(handwritten in margin: Vocab. Quiz)

7 Work and Lifestyles

> Success in life has nothing to do with what you gain in life or accomplish for yourself. It's what you do for others.
>
> Danny Thomas
> American entertainer

In Part 1, you will learn about different things that volunteers can do and who they can help. In the rest of this chapter, you will read about, explore, and discuss personal volunteer experiences and volunteering around the world.

Connecting to the Topic

1. Describe the photo. What do you think these men and women are doing?

2. What do you think these volunteers are building? Why?

3. What other things can people do to help those in need?

Volunteering

Before You Read

1 **Thinking About the Topic** Look at the photos and discuss the questions.

1. What are five things that you see in each photo?
2. Who are these people?
3. What are they doing? Why?

▲ "Can I get you anything?"

▲ "Would you like some soup?"

◀ "Let's plant it here."

2 **Previewing Vocabulary** Read the words and phrases below. Listen to their pronunciation. Do not look them up in a dictionary. Put a check mark (✓) next to the words that you don't know.

Nouns	**Verbs**	**Adjectives**
▪ AIDS	▪ delivering (deliver)	▪ famous
▪ environment		▪ homeless
▪ hardships	▪ planted (plant)	▪ lonely
▪ homelessness	▪ prepare	
▪ lives (life)	▪ release	**Adverb**
▪ mammals	▪ volunteer	▪ daily
▪ teenagers		
▪ volunteers		**Expression**
		▪ take care of

Strategy

Finding the Meaning of New Words: Looking at Colons
You do not always need to use a dictionary to find the meaning of a new word. Sometimes a colon (:) can help you to understand a new word. If you know the key word or words on *one* side of the colon, then you can figure out the meaning of the word or words on the *other* side of the colon.

Examples
There are terrible **afflictions**: AIDS, cancer, and TB.

What are some examples of afflictions? *AIDS, cancer,* and *TB*

She cooked some wonderful foods: **stews**, **casseroles**, and **soufflés.**

What are stews, casseroles, and soufflés? *some wonderful foods*

3 **Finding the Meaning of New Words** The meaning of these words is in the next reading. Find the words and look before or after the colons for their meanings. Underline the meanings.

cypress	eucalyptus	pine	sea lions
elm	hardships	seals	sea otters

Read

4 **Reading an Article** Read the following article. Don't use your dictionary. If you don't know some words, try to figure out their meanings. Then do the activities.

Volunteering

A   Some people go to work each day and then come home. They spend time with their family and friends. Maybe they watch TV or go to a movie. Sometimes they exercise or read. This is their life. But for other people, this isn't enough. They look around their neighborhoods and see people with terrible **hardships:** sickness, loneliness, and **homelessness**. Other   5 people see problems with the environment. Many people want to help. They **volunteer**. They give some of their time to help others.

B   **Volunteers** help in many ways. Some visit sick and **lonely** people. Some give their friendship to children without parents. Some build houses for **homeless** people. Others sit and hold babies with **AIDS**.   10

C   Andy Lipkis was at summer camp when he **planted** his first tree. He began to think about the **environment**. In many countries, people were cutting down trees. Andy Lipkis worried about this. In 1974, he started a group, TreePeople, to plant trees: pine, elm, cypress, and eucalyptus. They also began to plant fruit trees in poor neighborhoods because fresh   15 fruit is often too expensive for poor people. Today there are thousands of members of TreePeople, and more join every day. They plant millions of trees everywhere to help the environment *and* people.

D   Ruth Brinker wasn't planning to change the world. Then a young friend became sick. He had AIDS. Soon he was very sick, and he couldn't   20 **take care of** himself. Brinker and other friends began to help him. In 1985, Brinker started Project Open Hand. This group cooks meals and takes them to people with   25 AIDS. Soon Project Open Hand volunteers were cooking many meals every day and **delivering** them to people who couldn't leave   30 home. Today, volunteers **prepare** 2,000 meals **daily**. Ruth Brinker didn't plan to change the world, but she is making a change in   35 people's **lives**.

▲ Caring for a sick seal

E   Only three volunteers began the Marine Mammal Center in northern California in 1975. Today there are 800 volunteers. They work with **mammals**. Mammals are animals that feed on their mother's milk when young. The volunteers help sick ocean mammals: seals, sea lions, and sea otters. The sick animals become well and strong. Motherless baby animals grow big and healthy. For many weeks—or sometimes months—volunteers help to feed and take care of these animals. They also work in an educational program that teaches people about these animals. The volunteers don't get any pay for their hard work. Their "pay" is the good feeling on the day when they can **release a** healthy animal—take it to its home, the ocean, and let it go free.   45

F   Thirty or forty years ago, most volunteers were housewives. They volunteered time while their husbands were working. Today both men and women volunteer—and **teenagers** and children, too. There are volunteers from all social classes, all neighborhoods, and all ages. Most aren't rich or **famous**. They enjoy their volunteer work. People need them. Today, the world needs volunteers more than ever before. Perhaps a young Zulu boy from South Africa, Nkosi Johnson, said it best. Before he died of AIDS at the age of 12, he made a speech that is now famous. In this speech, he said, "Do all you can with what you have, in the time you have, in the place you are."   60

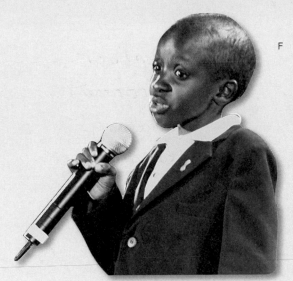
▲ Nkosi Johnson—small body, big heart

After You Read

5 Identifying the Main Ideas and Important Details Fill in this chart with information from the reading.

Name of the Organization	Who started it?	What do the volunteers do?	In which paragraph is this information?
TreePeople	Andy Lipkis	Plant trees + fruit trees	C
Project Open Hand	Ruth Brinker	Cook meals + take them to ppl w/ Aids or who can't leave thr homes	D
Marine Mammal Center	3 volunteers	Help sick marine animals	E

6 **Checking Vocabulary** Look back at the reading for the answers to these questions. (Look before or after the colons.)

1. What are three hardships? _Sickness, loneliness, homelessness_
2. What are pine, elm, cypress, and eucalyptus? _trees_
3. What are seals, sea lions, and sea otters? _mammals_

Now write the word for the meanings below. For help, look back at the boldfaced words in the reading.

Paragraph	Meaning	Word
A	give time to help others	_volunteer_
C	the place around us	_environment_
D	taking things to people	_delivering_
E	let an animal go free	_release_
F	people between 13 and 19 years old	_teenagers_

FOCUS

Sentence Structure: Understanding Sentences with the Word *That*
Sometimes a writer puts two sentences together with the word *that*.

Example

They found a sick seal. + It was on the beach.

They found a sick seal **that** was on the beach.

---

7 **Understanding Sentences with the Word *That*** Look back at Paragraph E to find a sentence with the word *that* for each pair of sentences below. Write the sentence on the lines.

1. Mammals are animals. ~~They~~ _that_ feed on their mother's milk when young.

_____

_____

2. They also work in an educational program. ~~It~~ _that_ teaches people about these animals.

_____

_____

Culture Note

Finding Places to Volunteer

Some people want to help others, but they wonder, "How can I find a place to volunteer?" In the United States, there is an organization called Volunteer Match. A person can go to their website, or other similar websites, and answer three questions:

- What is your zip code (area of the country in which you live)?
- How far can you travel to volunteer (how many miles)?
- What kind of volunteer work do you want to do? (Some possible answers are *animals, arts and culture, children, education, homeless people, and hunger.*)

The website will give you a list of many organizations in your area. Are there websites like this in other countries that you know about?

8 Discussing the Reading Discuss your answers to the following questions with a group.

1. Are any of the organizations in the reading interesting to you? If so, which one(s)? Why?

2. Do you (or does anyone you know) volunteer for any organization now, or did you in the past? Describe the organization and your experience volunteering.

PART 2   Main Ideas and Details

My Special Year

Before You Read

1 Thinking About the Topic Look at the photos on page 120. Answer the questions with a partner.

1. These are photos of the same city. There are big contrasts—differences—between them. Describe the neighborhoods and the people. How are they different? Use adjectives.

2. All cities have good areas and bad areas. What are some contrasts in *your* city? Discuss two neighborhoods that are very different from each other. Use adjectives.

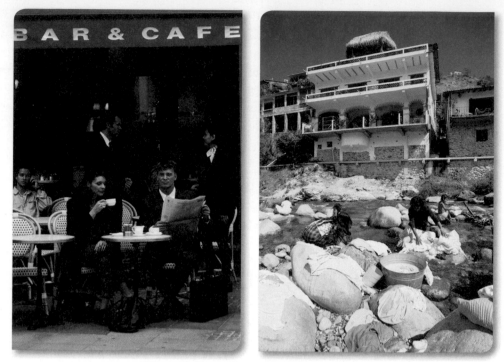

▲ What is life like for the people in these photos? ▲

2 Previewing Vocabulary Read the words below. Listen to their pronunciation. Do not look them up in a dictionary. Put a check mark (✓) next to the words that you don't know.

Nouns
- ▣ contrast ▣ energy
- ▣ crime ▣ street children
- ▣ drugs

Verbs
- ▣ email
- ▣ taught (teach)

Adjectives
- ▣ fun
- ▣ tough

Read

3 Reading a Narrative Read the narrative. Then answer the questions.

My Special Year

A   My name is Pablo. I think I'm a lucky guy. I have a good family, and we live in a nice neighborhood in a really special place, Puerto Vallarta, Mexico. People travel here from many countries for their vacations. We have beautiful beaches, hotels, restaurants, shopping, and sports.

B   However, in my beautiful hometown, there are also very poor   5
neighborhoods. These areas are crowded and have a lot of **crime**. Life is terrible for many of the children in these areas. Some don't really have a

childhood because they're homeless and live on the streets. They don't have families or education. They don't have enough food. Most of them have chronic stress. Many use **drugs** or have diseases or mental problems.

C   Last year, I came back to Puerto Vallarta from my university in Mexico City. I spent one year as a volunteer with an organization called Outreach International. They have several programs. I volunteered for one program to help **street children**. It was the best—and most difficult—year of my life. I learned a lot that year.

D   I worked in a home for street children (all boys at this one). It's in an old school that nobody uses now. At this home, the boys have a place to sleep and three meals daily, but it's not a school. (They go to a neighborhood school.) The home keeps the boys off the streets. It shows them another way of life. As a volunteer, I helped to prepare meals. I **taught** games—such as basketball and football—and art. I helped the kids with their homework. These kids can be **fun**. They have a lot of **energy**, but they're also really **tough**. Their hardships on the streets make them strong and not always "sweet little children."

E   At this boys' home, I met two other volunteers—Brian from Canada and Greg from Australia. In many ways, we were very similar. We were the same age, came from good homes, had a good education, and liked to travel. They were both college students, like me. We became friends. I helped them with Spanish, and they helped me with English. They came to meet my family, and we had fun together. Now, we **email** each other. But more than anything, I will always remember the children. I hope their lives can be better in the future. The **contrast** between their lives and my life is big. I hope they can have a good life, like I do.

After You Read

Strategy

Organizing Details Using a T-chart

In the reading, there were several contrasts and many details. You can use a T-chart to organize two sides of a topic.

Traveling

Good Things About It	Bad Things About It
fun	expensive
learn about new places	tiring
meet new people	miss home

4 Organizing Details Using a T-chart Complete the chart about Puerto Vallarta.

Puerto Vallarta

Good Things About It	Bad Things About It
beautiful beaches sports	crime homeless children

5 Organizing Details On a separate sheet of paper make a T-chart to show the differences between the lives of the volunteers and the lives of the street children.

6 Thinking Critically: Making Inferences Read the sentences below. They are from the reading. Make guesses about street children from these sentences. Discuss your answers with a small group.

1. I worked in a home for these street children (all boys at this one).

   What can you guess?

   Ⓐ The street children were happy at the home.

   Ⓑ Only boys live on the street.

   Ⓒ There is a different home for girls.

   Ⓓ I got money for my work.

2. These kids can be fun. They have a lot of energy, but they're also really *tough*. Their hardships on the streets make them strong and not always "sweet little children."

   What can you guess about the word *tough*? It means:

   Ⓐ fun and with a lot of energy

   Ⓑ strong

   Ⓒ sweet little children

   Ⓓ strong and not sweet

Strategy

Understanding Words from Their Parts: Suffixes

The ending of some words can help you with the meaning. These endings are called *suffixes*. Here are two: *-less* and *-ness*.

Word Ending and Meaning	Example
• *-less* means "without"; words with *-less* are adjectives	home**less** (= with no home)
• *-ness* means "a condition of"; words with *-ness* are nouns	homeless**ness** (= the condition of not having a home) happi**ness** (= the condition of being happy)

7 **Understanding Words from Their Parts: Suffixes** Write an adjective with the suffix *-less* on each line. Compare your answers with a partner's.

1. The gum doesn't have sugar. It is _____*sugarless*_____.

2. He doesn't have a job. He is _____*jobless*_____.

3. They don't have hope. They are _____*hopeless*.

4. He doesn't have a friend. He is _____*friendless*_____.

5. She didn't get any sleep last night. It was a _____*sleepless*_____ night.

6. He doesn't have a heart. (He doesn't care about people.) He is _____*heartless*_____.

7. The baby seal doesn't have a mother. She is _____*motherless*.

8 **Understanding Words from Their Parts: Suffixes** Now write the correct words from the box on the following lines. Follow the example. (One word will not be used.)

home	homeless	homelessness
hope	hopeless	hopelessness
power	powerless	powerlessness

1. John lost his _____*home*_____. _____*Homelessness*_____ is a big

problem in this city, and he felt very unhappy because he was

_____*homeless*_____.

2. When people become homeless they often lose _hope_____
   for the future. They begin to feel __hopeless_____.
   hopelessness is a big problem for people living on the streets.

3. A sick person with no money often feels _powerless___. This
   powerlessness can cause depression and sadness.

9 **Discussing the Reading** Discuss your answers to the following questions.

1. What are some problems that street children (in any country) might have?
   Make a list.

2. In your opinion, is the situation hopeless? Why or why not?

3. What can we do to help poor people? List five things.

10 **Writing in Your Journal** Choose one topic below. Write about it for five
minutes. Use some of the vocabulary that you learned in this chapter.

- the problems of street children
- your ideas on how to help poor people
- one time when you were a volunteer
- one of the organizations from this chapter: TreePeople, Project Open Hand,
  The Marine Mammal Center, Outreach International.

PART 3 | Practical English

Reading Charts

1 **Reading a Chart** Read the information below and look at the chart about
eleven countries on page 125. Answer the questions that follow.

> The chart lists the percentage of people who volunteer in each country. It also
> lists information about the value of what each country produced in one year. This
> is called the Gross National Product (GNP). The GNP per person is a country's
> yearly income divided by the population. See this example:
>   GNP = $5,000,000,000
>   Population: 50,000,000
>   GNP per person = $5,000,000,000 ÷ 50,000,000 = $100.00

Country	Percent of Population Volunteering	GNP Per Person
Brazil	12%	U.S. $4,630
Colombia	48	2,470
Finland	33	24,280
France	23	24,210
Germany	26	26,570
Israel	12	16,180
Japan	9	32,350
Netherlands	46	24,780
Sweden	51	25,580
Spain	12	14,100
U.S.	49	29,240

1. Which country has the highest percentage of volunteering? _Sweden_

2. Which country is the richest? _Japan_

3. Which country is richer, Germany or Spain? _Germ_

4. Which four countries have the lowest percentage of volunteering?
   Brazi, Israel, Jap, Spain

5. Which country has a higher percentage of volunteers, Finland or Spain?
   Finland

6. Which countries have four times the volunteers of Israel? _Colombia, the U.S. Sweden_

Discuss with a group what you notice about the answers. Is anything surprising?

2 **Working with Averages** The average GNP per person for the 11 countries on the chart is about $20,339. (The total amount of the GNP divided by the 11 countries.)

Germany is $6,231 above the average ($26,570 – $20,339 = $6,231), which is about 30 percent. Answer these questions about the chart.

1. How much above the average is Sweden? $ _5241_
   (which is about 27% above)

2. How much below the average is Brazil? $ _15,709_
   (which is about 77% below)

3. What country is closest to the average? _France_

4. Which country is most above the average? _Jap_ How much? _12,011_

5. Which country is the most below the average? _Colombia_ How much? _17,869_

6. What is the average rate of volunteering among these eleven countries? _approx. 29_

1 **Building Vocabulary** The underlined words below are from this chapter. Circle the word in each group that does not belong or relate to the vocabulary word.

1.	volunteer	work	(money)	help
2.	tough	(weak)	strong	not nice
3.	plant	(cut down)	grow	food
4.	email	(travel)	computer	website
5.	street children	(lucky)	poor	hungry
6.	daily	weekly	(early)	monthly
7.	young	child	childhood	(sick)
8.	energy	power	(weakness)	strength
9.	teach	educate	(learn)	show
10.	drugs	(coffee)	pills	medicine
11.	famous	(unknown)	popular	well known
12.	fruit	lemon	(carrot)	banana
13.	fun	enjoyable	(boring)	happy
14.	lonely	(cheerful)	alone	by oneself

2 **Listening: Focusing on High-Frequency Words** Listen and fill in the missing words below.

Ruth Brinker wasn't planning to ___change___ the world. Then a
___young___ friend became sick. He had AIDS. Soon he was very

sick, and he couldn't ___take___ care of himself. Brinker and other

friends ___began___ to help him. In 1985, Brinker started Project

Open Hand. This ___group___ cooks meals and takes them to

people with AIDS. Soon Project Open Hand volunteers were cooking many

meals every day and delivering them to people who couldn't leave home.

Today, volunteers ___prepare___ 2,000 meals ___daily___.

Ruth Brinker didn't plan to change the ___world___, but she is

making a change in people's ___lives___.

3 **Working with Vocabulary** Use the words in the box to complete the new paragraph about a kind man.

AIDS	hardships	homelessness	volunteering
crime	homeless	volunteer	volunteers

George works hard but he still finds time to ___volunteer___ [1]. He ___volunteers___ [2] at a church in the middle of the city. There is a lot of ___crime___ [3], like robbery and drug selling, so it is dangerous. There is also a lot of ___homelessness___ [4], and people sleep on the street. The ___homeless___ [5] people have terrible ___hardships___ [6]. Some have diseases like ___AIDS___ [7]. George is ___volunteering___ [8] because he wants to make a difference.

▲ A volunteer sign-up sheet

4 **Building Vocabulary** Complete the crossword puzzle with words from the box. These words are from Chapters 6 and 7.

AIDS	fruit	mammal	symbol
awake	hardships	plant	taught
contrast	homeless	release	tough
emotions	logic	research	vision
famous	lonely	rich	volunteer

Across

2. strong and able to take care of yourself (adj.)

4. examples: a human, a seal, or a dog (n.)

6. a big or strong difference (n.)

9. close, careful study of something (n.)

13. Scientists and mathematicians use this when they think. (n.)

14. with no home (adj.)

15. work for free (v.)

18. You do this to a tree or a seed. (v.)

19. Everybody knows about you; you are _____. (adj.)

20. examples: love, anxiety, joy (n.)

Down

1. a very serious disease (n.)

3. problems in life (n.)

5. When you're not sleeping, you're _____. (adj.)

7. the past tense of *teach* (v.)

8. examples: a lemon, an orange, a banana (n.)

10. examples: a flag or a red cross (n.)

11. the opposite of poor (adj.)

12. without any friends (adj.)

16. let something go (v.)

17. what you have because of your eyes (n.)

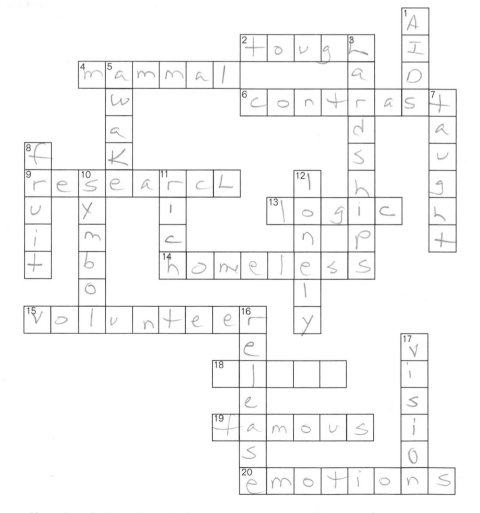

Key: *adj.* = adjective; *adv.* = adverb; *n.* = noun; *prep.* = preposition; *v.* = verb

Self-Assessment Log

Read the lists below. Check (✓) the strategies and vocabulary that you learned in this chapter.. Look through the chapter or ask your instructor about the strategies and words that you do not understand.

Reading and Vocabulary-Building Strategies
- ☐ Finding the meaning of new words: looking at colons
- ☐ Identifying the main ideas and important details
- ☐ Understanding sentences with the word *that*
- ☐ Organizing details using a T-chart
- ☐ Making inferences
- ☐ Understanding words from their parts: suffixes
- ☐ Reading a chart

Target Vocabulary

Nouns
- ☐ AIDS
- ☐ contrast
- ☐ crime
- ☐ drugs
- ☐ energy*
- ☐ environment
- ☐ hardships
- ☐ homelessness
- ☐ lives* (life)*
- ☐ mammals
- ☐ street* children*
- ☐ teenagers
- ☐ volunteers
- ☐ world*

Verbs
- ☐ delivering
- ☐ email
- ☐ planted*
- ☐ prepare*
- ☐ release
- ☐ taught (teach)
- ☐ volunteer

Adjectives
- ☐ famous*
- ☐ fun*
- ☐ homeless
- ☐ lonely
- ☐ tough

Adverb
- ☐ daily

Expression
- ☐ take* care* of*

* These words are among the 1,000 most-frequently used words in English.

CHAPTER 8

Food and Nutrition

"I've been on a diet for two weeks, and all I've lost is two weeks."

Totie Fields
American comedian

write in Ntbk: *On board: My favorite food is _____*

wly?

In this CHAPTER

In Part 1, you will read about how people are changing their way of eating. In this rest of the chapter, you will read about, discuss, and explore unusual foods, diets, and nutrition.

Connecting to the Topic

1. What is the family doing? What do you think they are saying?
2. What foods do you see in the photo?
3. What are four foods that you like to cook?

eggs
soups + beans
vegetables
pasta + rice dishes

New Foods, New Diets

Before You Read

*Get up &
ask 4 students:*

1 **Interviewing Other Students** Look at the questions in the chart below. Decide on your answers. Then walk around the room and ask four students the two questions. Write their answers in this chart.

Question	Student 1	Student 2	Student 3	Student 4
1. What foods do people eat now that people didn't eat 500 years ago?	*Pizza*	*Junk food rice*	*Pizza*	*Eggs fret*
2. Are the foods that we eat now *more* or *less* healthy than 500 years ago?		*not really*		*less healthy*

Strategy

Previewing a Reading
Before you read something, look it over quickly. Look at the pictures and read the titles and the headings (the titles for each paragraph or section). This will give you ideas about the reading. With ideas in mind, you will understand more.

2 **Previewing a Reading** Read the questions below. Answer them with a partner by previewing the reading.

1. What are the four headings? — *go to 134*
   Diet of the Past _____

   _____ _____

2. Look at the pictures. What are the people doing?

3. What will the reading be about?

3 **Previewing Vocabulary** Read the words below. Listen to their pronunciation. Do not look them up in a dictionary. Put a check mark (✓) next to the words that you don't know.

Nouns	Verbs	Adjectives	Conjunction
▦ centers	▦ gain	▦ attractive	▦ while
▦ diabetes	▦ join	▦ dairy	
▦ diet	▦ spend	▦ fried	
▦ irony		▦ raw	
▦ obesity		▦ slim	
▦ Rubens		▦ ugly	
▦ thousands			
▦ Titian			

Strategy

Using Opposites to Understand a New Word
Sometimes you can understand a new word if you know its opposite. If you know one of these words, you may not need a dictionary for the other.

Example
The people in the first picture aren't thin; they're **overweight**.
(The opposite of *thin* is *overweight*.)

4 **Using Opposites to Understand a New Word** Read the sentences. Then write the opposite of the underlined word.

1. People thought, "How <u>attractive</u>!"—not, "How ugly!"

   The opposite of *attractive* is _____ugly_____.

2. Many of the vegetables are <u>raw</u>. They aren't cooked because cooking takes away some vitamins.

   The opposite of *raw* is _____cooked_____.

3. People these days want to be <u>slim</u>, not fat.

   The opposite of *slim* is _____fat_____.

4. Sometimes people lose weight fast, but they usually <u>gain</u> it back again.

   The opposite of *gain* is _____lose_____.

Read

5 **Reading an Article** Read the following article. Don't use your dictionary. If you don't know some words, try to figure out their meanings. Then do the activities.

New Foods, New Diets

Diet of the Past

A   On March 26, 1662, Samuel Pepys and four friends had lunch at his home in London, England. They ate beef, cheese, two kinds

▲ A painting by Bruegel

of fish, and six chickens. Today, we might wonder, "What? No fruits? No vegetables?" More than 300 years ago, people in Europe ate differently from today. They looked different, too. In famous paintings by Bruegel, Rubens, and other artists, people weren't thin; they were overweight. But people 300 years ago thought, "How **attractive**!"— not, "How **ugly**!"

Today's Diet

B   Today, people are learning more about health. Many people are changing their ways of eating. They're eating a lot of fruits and vegetables. Many of the vegetables are **raw**. They aren't cooked because cooking takes away some vitamins, such as vitamins A, B, and C. People are eating less sugar. They're eating low-fat foods. They're not eating much red meat. They're drinking less cola and coffee.

▲ People exercising in a modern health club

Trying to Be Thin

C   People these days want to be **slim**, not fat. Sometimes people in North America go a little crazy to lose pounds. **Thousands** of them **join** gyms and diet groups, go to special diet doctors, or **spend** a lot of money at diet **centers**. Each year Americans spend more than $46 billion on diets and diet products.

More People Are Overweight

D   However, there is an **irony**—a surprising, opposite result—to all this dieting. **While** many people are becoming thin, other people are becoming overweight. *More* people are *overweight* than in the past! In many countries, there is a serious problem with **obesity**—in other words, a condition of being very overweight. There are two main reasons. First, these days, many people often go to fast-food restaurants. (They didn't in the past.) At these restaurants, many of the foods (such as **fried** potatoes and meat) are high in fat. Some of the **dairy** products (such as cheese) are high in fat, and others (such as ice cream) are high in fat *and* sugar. This seems similar to Samuel Pepys's party, doesn't it? Second, dieting doesn't often work. Sometimes people lose weight

5

10

15

20

25

30

35

fast, but they usually **gain** it back again. Almost 95 percent of all people gain back weight after a diet. One problem with obesity is easy to see: overweight people have more sicknesses, such as heart disease and **diabetes**.

40

E   Sometimes people go crazy over food. Sometimes they eat very little because they want to be slim. Other times, they eat lots of bad foods because these foods taste good. When will people learn? Too much food, too little food, and the wrong foods are all bad ideas.

Culture Note

Vegetarians

Vegetarians are people who don't eat meat. Some vegetarians don't eat dairy products, either. In what countries or cultures is it easy to be a vegetarian? In what countries or cultures is it hard? If you are a vegetarian, why did you decide to be one? If you are not a vegetarian, would you consider becoming one? Why or why not?

After You Read

6 Identifying the Topics Read the topics below. Which paragraph is about each topic? Write the letter of the paragraph next to its topic.

1. __C__ spending a lot of time and money on diets
2. __A__ how people in Europe ate in the past
3. __E__ conclusion
4. __D__ a serious problem with weight in some countries
5. __B__ foods for good health

7 Working with New Words Write the vocabulary words for the meanings below. For help, look back at the boldfaced words in the reading.

Paragraph	Meaning	Vocabulary Word
D	at the same time	while
D	a surprising, opposite result	irony
D	a word for products from milk	dairy
D	a condition of being very overweight	obesity
A	two famous painters	Bruegal + Rubens
D	a sickness	diabetes

Strategy

Organizing Details

When you organize notes and show the relationship of details, you can use graphic organizers like this one.

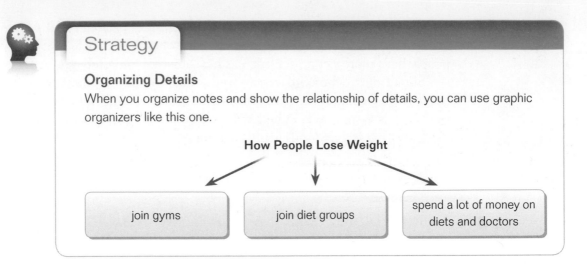

How People Lose Weight

| join gyms | join diet groups | spend a lot of money on diets and doctors |

8 **Finding Reasons** Look back at Paragraph D on page 134. Why are many people overweight these days? Find two reasons. Write them in the boxes below.

Reasons for Obesity Today

Many ppl eat at fast food rest.

Dieting often doesn't work

Strategy

Figuring Out Words with More Than One Meaning

Many words in English have two or more meanings. Use the context to understand which meaning is correct in the sentence or paragraph where it is used.

Examples

I shouldn't eat all of this food. I'm on a **diet**.

   (Here, *diet* means eating less food than usual.)

A sea lion's **diet** is mostly fish.

   (Here, *diet* means the food that a person or animal usually eats.)

9 **Figuring Out Words with More Than One Meaning** What does the verb *work* mean in each sentence? Choose the best answer for each sentence.

1. I have to <u>work</u> hard to stay thin.

   Ⓐ have a job

   Ⓑ be active and try

   Ⓒ succeed

2. Dieting often doesn't <u>work</u>. People usually gain back the weight.

    Ⓐ have a job

    Ⓑ be active and try

    Ⓒ succeed

3. They <u>work</u> in the entertainment business.

    Ⓐ have a job

    Ⓑ be active and try

    Ⓒ succeed

 10 Discussing the Reading Fill in the chart below about a culture that you know well. Then talk about It with a partner.

Meal	What do people usually eat and drink?	Are these different from foods in the past?
Breakfast	bread waffles pancakes eggs cereal fruit, juice bacon + sausage coffee tea	no
Lunch	a sandwich	yes, meals at\from home
Dinner	pasta chicken salads beef fish ethnic foods vegetables	yes, more meat + pot

PART 2   Main Ideas and Details

Eating Bugs

Before You Read

 1 Previewing the Reading Look at the photos in the reading on pages 138–139. What will the reading probably be about?

2 Interviewing Other Students Look at the questions in the chart on the next page. Decide on your answers. Then walk around the room and ask three students the same questions. Write their answers in the chart.

Questions	Student 1	Student 2	Student 3
1. What are two of your favorite foods?			
2. Imagine that you can eat only one food for the rest of your life. What is it?			
3. What food do you dislike?			
4. What is one expensive, gourmet food that you like?			

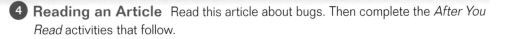

3 **Previewing Vocabulary** Read the words below. Listen to their pronunciation. Do not look them up in a dictionary. Put a check mark (✓) next to the words that you don't know.

Nouns	**Verbs**	**Adjectives**	**Conjunction**
▢ Asians	▢ bake	▢ delicious	▢ except
▢ bugs	▢ boil	▢ disgusting	
▢ entomologists	▢ disgusts		
▢ insects	▢ fry	**Adverb**	
▢ protein	▢ marinate	▢ worldwide	
▢ snacks			

Read

4 **Reading an Article** Read this article about bugs. Then complete the *After You Read* activities that follow.

Eating Bugs

A   Different cultures enjoy different foods. Sometimes a food that one culture thinks is **delicious** might seem **disgusting** to another. In much of the world, people eat beef, but the idea of meat from a cow **disgusts** some Hindus in India. People in France sometimes eat horsemeat or frogs, and this disgusts some Americans. People in Western countries eat cheese, and many **Asians** think that this is disgusting. And then there are

5

▲ A grasshopper

insects. Many people wonder, "How can people eat *bugs*?" (Children in the U.S. make horrible faces and say, "Ooooh! Yucky!") However, insects are an important part of the diets in many countries.

10

15

▲ An ant

B   In different places, people eat over 1,000 types of insects—and ate them in the past, too. For example, people in ancient Greece and Rome ate insects. American Indians ate grasshoppers, crickets, and caterpillars. Today, in parts of Africa, people eat termites (insects that eat wood) and caterpillars as **snacks**. In Japan, some people eat grasshoppers with soy sauce. In small villages and in some restaurants in Thailand, people enjoy crickets and grasshoppers. In some Mexican restaurants, people pay $25 for a plate of butterfly larvae. In the United States, some restaurants now offer insects as a gourmet food. In China, people spend $100 million each year on ants.

20

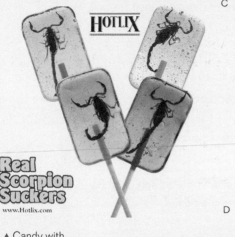

▲ Candy with insects

C   There are different ways to prepare bugs as food. One way is to **boil** them in very hot water. In Colombia, some people spread them on bread. In the Philippines, people **fry** them in butter with vegetables. In Mexico, people fry them in oil or **marinate** them in lemon juice, salt, and chile. In some parts of Africa, some people **bake** or fry them. In other areas, they eat them raw. (However, **entomologists**—scientists who study insects—say that it's important to cook insects, not eat them raw.) In the United States, a company called Hotlix now sells *candy* with insects in it.

25

30

D   Julieta Ramos-Elorduy, a researcher at a university in Mexico City, says that there are many good reasons to eat **bugs**. First, insects are a cheap food (**except** on a plate in an expensive restaurant), and they taste good. Some insects taste like nuts, bacon, mint or cinnamon. Second, bugs are good for our health. For example, they often have more **protein** than beef or fish. Third, they can bring money to poor people, who find them in the forest and sell them. In parts of Africa, there are seven pounds of insects on just one tree. This brings a good profit for very little work. Finally, eating insects can help to save the environment. In many countries, people cut down trees. However, they will not do this if the trees have insects to eat or sell.

35

40

45

A caterpillar ▶

E   People **worldwide** are now eating foods from other countries. People in the West now enjoy Japanese sushi (a small roll of cooked white rice wrapped around raw fish, vegetables, or egg). People everywhere eat Italian pizza and American hamburgers. Maybe someday, in a fast-food restaurant in any country, a customer will say, "Give me a hamburger and an order of caterpillars, please." In the future, insects might be as familiar to us as rice, bread, or beans.

50

After You Read

Strategy

Read ← (handwritten)

Finding the Main Ideas in a Reading

? Where do you find... (handwritten)

The main idea of a whole reading is usually in the first paragraph—the introduction. After that, each paragraph has a main idea, too, often in its first sentence. The last paragraph is the conclusion. It usually has one sentence that "finishes" the reading and might suggest a new idea, too.

What ds the con do? (handwritten)

5 **Identifying the Main Ideas** Read the main ideas below. Look back at the reading for the paragraph that expresses each of the main ideas. Then write the letter of the paragraph next to the main idea. Which of these ideas is the main idea of the whole reading? Put a check in front of that sentence.

1. _D_ There are many reasons to eat insects.
2. _B_ People in many countries eat insects.
3. _A_ Foods such as insects are delicious to some people and not to others.
4. _E_ In the future, people might eat insects everywhere, and they won't think it's strange.
5. _C_ People prepare and eat insects in different ways.

6 **Finding Details: Reasons** Look back at Paragraph D on page 139. What are four reasons to eat insects? Write them in the boxes.

Reasons to eat insects:

- Insects are cheap + they taste good
- They're good for health
- They bring $ to poor ppl
- Eating them helps save the environment

7 **Finding Details** Look back at the reading to find the answers to these questions.

1. In Paragraph C, how many ways can you find to prepare insects to eat? Write the ways on a piece of paper. *8*

2. In the whole reading, how many types of insects can you find? Write their names on a piece of paper. *6*

8 **Checking Vocabulary** Fill in the blanks with words from the box.

bugs	entomologists	protein
disgusting	except	worldwide

1. In the past, only the Japanese ate sushi. Now, people ___*worldwide*___ eat it.

2. My little boy didn't want to eat the meat because he thought it was ___*disgusting*___, but we told him it was really very good.

3. Meat, fish, and insects have a lot of ___*protein*___, and this is necessary for good health.

4. ___*Except*___ for Hindus, people in most cultures eat some amount of beef.

5. ___*Entomologists*___ study caterpillars, grasshoppers, ants, and other ___*bugs*___.

9 **Discussing the Reading** Discuss your answers to the following questions.

1. Is there some food from your culture that you think is disgusting? If so, what is it?
2. Do you eat anything that other people think is strange?
3. What is the strangest food that you have ever eaten?

10 **Writing in Your Journal** Choose one topic below. Write about it for five minutes. Use some of the vocabulary that you learned in this chapter.

- something that you learned about food
- your opinion of diets
- your opinion of eating insects
- the strangest thing that you have ever eaten

Reading Charts

1 **Reading a Food Chart** Look at the following chart. It lists the fat and calories in eleven types of food.

1. Which food has the most calories? _____

2. Which food has the least calories? _____

3. Circle the foods that you like.

Reading Tip

calorie: a unit to measure the amount of energy food will produce

Food Item	Calories	Fat (in grams)
apple (1)	80	.0
beef steak (3 oz.)	242	14.7
broccoli (3 1/2 oz.)	25	.2
chicken (baked leg)	130	4.7
chocolate chip cookie (1)	48	2
French fries (one serving)	200	10.0
grapes (1 bunch)	51	.1
milk (1 glass)	149	8.1
popcorn (2 cups, with butter)	85	12
potato chips (11)	140	11.0
tomato juice (small glass)	41	.1

2 **Reading a Chart** Look at the two pictures below and answer the questions about Bill and Maria. Use the food chart above.

▲ Bill is eating dinner.　　　　▲ Maria is eating dinner.

1. How many calories does Bill's steak have?

2. How much fat does it have? (How many grams of fat?)

3. How many calories do Bill's French fries have?

4. How much fat do Bill's French fries have? (How many grams?) _____ 10

5. How many calories does Bill's complete meal have? _____ 735

6. How much fat does it have? (How many grams?) _____ 38.8

7. How many calories does Maria's chicken have? _____ 130

8. How much fat does it have? (How many grams of fat?) _____ 4.7

9. How many calories do Maria's grapes have? _____ 51

10. How much fat do they have? (How many grams)? _____ .1

11. How many calories does Maria's complete dinner have? _____ 247

12. How much fat does it have? (How many grams?) _____ 5.1

13. You want to lose weight. Should you eat Maria's dinner or Bill's dinner?

_____

14. You want to eat less fat. Should you eat Bill's dinner or Maria's dinner?

_____

15. Bill's doctor wants Bill to eat about 500 calories for dinner. Create a dinner for Bill that is about 500 calories. What does it include?

Steak, french fries, broccoli, grapes
242   200   25   51

518

Steak, brocc, milk + an apple (496)

PART **4** Vocabulary Practice

① **Building Vocabulary** Read the words below. Circle the word in each line that does not belong in that group.

1. diabetes	heart disease	sickness	(health)
2. bugs	(birds)	insects	ants
3. overweight	(slim)	heavy	fat
4. boil	(lose)	bake	fry
5. protein	fat	(sushi)	calories
6. entomologist	scientist	(protein)	insect
7. (worldwide)	unattractive	not pretty	ugly
8. gain	add	(lose)	grow

② **Listening: Filling in the Missing Words** Listen and fill in the words from the reading on page 134. Some of the words are new and some of the words are not new. Then check your answers.

Food and Nutrition   **143**

Do you listen?

There is an irony—a surprising, _opposite_ result—
to all this dieting. While many people are _becoming_ thin, other
people are becoming overweight. _More_ people are *overweight*
than in the past! In many countries, there is a _serious_
problem with obesity—in other words, a _condition_ of being
very overweight. There are two main _reasons_. First, these
days, _many_ people often go to fast-food restaurants. (They
didn't in the _past_.) At these restaurants, many of the foods
(_such_ as fried potatoes and meat) are _high_
in fat. Some of the dairy _products_ (such as cheese) are
high in fat, and _others_ (such as ice cream) are high in fat
and _sugar_. This seems similar to Samuel Pepys's party,
doesn't it? Second, dieting doesn't often work. Sometimes
people _lose_ weight fast, but they usually _gain_
it back again. Almost 95 percent of all people _gain_ back
weight after a _diet_. One problem with _obesity_
is easy to see: overweight people have more _sicknesses_ such as
heart disease and diabetes.

3 **Reviewing Vocabulary** Read each sentence and write whether each
statement is *True* or *False*. When you finish, correct the false sentences.

1. Termites are <u>insects</u> that eat wood. _T_
2. Sushi usually contains <u>fried</u> fish. _F_
3. If you <u>fry</u> something, you usually put it in oil. _T_
4. If you <u>gain</u> weight, you will weigh less. _F_
5. Vegetables usually have a lot of <u>calories</u>. _F_
6. People often eat chicken <u>raw</u>. _F_
7. If you <u>boil</u> something, you cook it in water. _T_
8. Ice cream is a <u>dairy</u> product. _T_

4 Focusing on High-Frequency Words Read the paragraph below and fill in each blank with a word from the box.

centers	join	people	spend
diet	lose	sometimes	thousands

_____People_____ these days want to be slim, not fat. _____Sometimes_____
1   2
people in North America go a little crazy to _____lose_____ pounds.
3
_____Thousands_____ of them _____Joic_____ gyms and diet groups, go
4   5
to special _____diet_____ doctors, or spend a lot of money at diet
6
_____center_____. Each year Americans _____spend_____ more than $46
7   8
billion on diets and diet products.

5 Building Vocabulary Complete the crossword puzzle on page 146 with words from the box. These words are from Chapters 7 and 8.

Asians	delicious	irony	slim
attractive	disgusting	motherless	snack
boil	environment	obesity	teenager
bugs	healthy	protein	ugly
cows	insects	raw	volunteer

▲ Does eating insects sound yummy or disgusting to you?

Across

1. very hot water can do this (v.)
7. example: ants and crickets (n.)
10. the opposite of sick (adj.)
12. food that is uncooked (adj.)
13. condition of being very overweight (n.)
14. example: Chinese, Japanese, Koreans, Thai people (n.)
15. meat and fish have a lot of this (n.)
19. When you're 13 to 19 years old, you are a _____. (n.)
20. Old, rotten, and smelly food is _____. (adj.)

Down

2. a surprising and opposite thing (n.)
3. Hindus don't eat these. (n.)
4. to do work without pay (v.)
5. tasting very, very good (adj.)
6. opposite of beautiful (adj.)
8. the air, trees, ocean—everything around us (n.)
9. nice to look at (adj.)
11. without a mother (adj.)
16. a little bit to eat, often between meals (noun)
17. thin or not fat (adj.)
18. insects (noun)

Key: *adj.* = adjective; *adv.* = adverb; *n.* = noun; *prep.* = preposition; *v.* = verb

Self-Assessment Log

Read the lists below. Check (✓) the strategies and vocabulary that you learned in this chapter. Look through the chapter or ask your instructor about the strategies and words that you do not understand.

Reading and Vocabulary-Building Strategies

☐ Previewing a reading
☐ Using opposites to understand a new word
☐ Identifying the topics
☐ Organizing details using a graphic organizer
☐ Figuring out words with more than one meaning
☐ Identifying the main ideas in a reading
☐ Finding details: reasons
☐ Reading a chart

Target Vocabulary

Nouns	Verbs	Adjectives	Adverb
bugs	bake	attractive	worldwide
calories (calorie)	boil	dairy	
centers*	disgusts	delicious	**Conjunctions**
diabetes	fry	disgusting	except*
diet	gain	fried	while*
entomologists	join*	raw	
insects*	lose	slim	
irony	marinate	ugly	
obesity	spend		
people*			
protein			
snacks			
thousands*			

* These words are among the 1,000 most-frequently used words in English.

9 Great Destinations

> "Life is either a daring adventure or nothing."
>
> Helen Keller
> American writer

Get ready to think about vacations! In Part 1, you will read about adventure vacations. In the rest of this chapter, you will read about, discuss, and explore types of vacations, vacation tours, and the perfect vacation for you.

Connecting to the Topic

1 What country might this couple be in? What kind of vacation are they taking?

2 What are they looking at? What might they be saying to each other?

3 What kind of vacations do you enjoy?

Adventure Vacations

Before You Read

1 **Thinking About the Topic** First, look over the pictures. Then, with a small group, answer the questions below.

1. Where are these people on vacation? What are they doing?

2. Which of these activities do you enjoy? Why do you enjoy them?

3. What do people like to do on vacation? Read the list of examples on page 151. Write two more things. Then circle all of the things that *you* like to do on vacation.

▼ Camping

▼ Shopping

▲ Hiking

◄ Sightseeing

stay at a nice hotel	go to the movies or the theater
camp	meet new people
sightsee	learn new things
shop	_____
	_____

2 **Previewing the Reading** Look over the pictures and headings in the reading on pages 153–155. What kind of travel might this reading be about?

3 **Previewing Vocabulary** Read the words and phrases below. Listen to their pronunciation. Do not look them up in a dictionary. Put a check mark (✓) next to the words that you don't know.

Nouns
- adventure
- amount
- archaeologists
- behavior
- biologists
- climate
- coast
- dolphins
- evidence

- glaciers
- ocean
- plants
- pollution
- prehistory
- seeds
- sightseeing
- species
- weather

Verbs
- count
- disappearing
- go camping
- go sightseeing
- prefer

Adjectives
- bored
- intelligent
- tropical
- worried

Adverb
- together

4 **Working with New Words** Figure out the meaning of each underlined word from the context. Choose the best answer.

1. I don't like the <u>climate</u> in that part of the country. It's too hot in the summer and too cold in the winter.
   climate:
   - (A) cities
   - (B) summer activities
   - (C) weather conditions

2. My neighbors' children have very good <u>behavior</u>. They're active, but they don't make a lot of noise, and they're always polite.
   behavior:
   - (A) way of acting
   - (B) health
   - (C) school work

3. Many things cause pollution—for example, factory smoke in the air and garbage in the water.
pollution:

(A) rain and bad weather

(B) new business

(C) unhealthy things in the environment

4. There are twenty species of mammals, thirty-seven species of insects, and fifty-two species of plants in that area.
species:

(A) kinds of animals

(B) kinds of plants

(C) kinds of living things

5. My wife likes the desert. My children like rivers and lakes in the mountains. But I prefer the coast, especially in the summer, when I can go swimming.

prefer: coast:

(A) like   (A) cities

(B) swim   (B) ocean beaches

(C) dislike   (C) forests

6. Tropical places such as Hawaii and Malaysia are beautiful and full of color, but they can be very hot, too.
tropical:

(A) states in the United States

(B) islands in the ocean

(C) areas near the Equator (the circle around the Earth that separates north from south)

FOCUS

Understanding Words for Direction

We use direction words (north, south, east, west) to show the relationship of one area to another. If you know the words for the four basic directions, you can figure out four *other* directions. They are combinations of *north*, *south*, *east*, and *west*.

North

West   East

South

---

5 **Understanding New Words for Direction** Use the information in the box above to answer these questions about four *other* directions.

1. What is a word for the direction between south and west? _southwest_

2. What is a word for the direction between south and east? _SE_

3. What is a word for the direction between north and west? _NW_

4. What is a word for the direction between north and east? _NE_

6 **Reading an Article** Read the following article. Don't use your dictionary. If you don't know some words, try to figure out their meanings. Then do the activities.

Adventure Vacations

A People like different kinds of vacations. Some **go camping**. They swim, fish, cook over a fire, and sleep outside. Others like to stay at a hotel in an exciting city. They go shopping all day and go dancing all night. Or maybe they **go sightseeing** to places such as Disneyland in the United States, the Taj Mahal in India, or the Louvre in France. 5

A Different Kind of Vacation

B Some people are **bored** with sightseeing trips. They don't want to be "tourists." They **prefer** an **adventure**—a surprising and exciting trip. They want to learn something and maybe help people, too. How can they do this? Some travel companies and environmental groups are planning special adventures. Sometimes these trips are difficult, but they're a lot of fun. One 10 organization, Earthwatch, sends small groups of volunteers to different parts of the world. Some volunteers spend two weeks and study the environment. Others learn about people of the past. Others work with animals or **plants**.

Hard Work in the Far North

C Would you like an adventure in the Far North? Scientists are **worried** 15 about changes in the **climate** worldwide. They are studying how the environment is changing because of a warming climate. Two teams of volunteers (one in Alaska and the other in Iceland) will study 20 **glaciers**—huge fields of ice that move very slowly. These glaciers are getting smaller. Scientists wonder why and how. Another team will go to Manitoba, 25 Canada. This team will collect information on birds, mammals, and the **amount** of snow. If you like exercise and cold **weather**, these are good trips for you, but 30 you must be in very good physical condition.

▲ Collecting information

Studying Ocean Mammals

▲ Dolphins are intelligent ocean mammals.

Do you enjoy **ocean** animals? You can spend two weeks in Florida. There you can study **dolphins**. It will be exciting to 35 learn about these **intelligent** ocean mammals. These beautiful animals can live to over 50 years of age. They travel **together** in family groups. From small 40 boats, volunteers will study and photograph these groups. The purpose of this research is to learn about the animals' social **behavior**. Scientists want to know 45 what dolphins do and how they live. Also, scientists want to study dolphins' health. For example, they wonder, "Is ocean **pollution** changing the dolphins' health?" 50 If you like warm weather, the ocean, and animals, this is a good trip for you.

Digging Up the Past

▲ Archaeologists dig up an area for evidence of the past.

Are you interested in history or **prehistory?** Then southwest France 55 is the place for your adventure. Between 35,000 and 50,000 years ago, early humans lived in this area. Volunteers will work with **archaeologists** from France, 60 Germany, and the United States to search for evidence about the way of life of the people from that time. If you choose this adventure, you will dig for stone tools and bones, clean 65 them, and photograph them. In your free time, you can travel around the beautiful countryside in the south of France.

▲ Biologists try to save plant species in Mexico.

Beaches and Biology

F   Do you enjoy the beach and like to learn about plants? There is an Earthwatch adventure in Yucatan, Mexico. On the north **coast** of Yucatan, there are beautiful **species** of plants. Unfortunately, many of them are **disappearing**. People dig them up and sell them for large amounts of money. Mexican **biologists** need volunteers to collect **seeds**, **count** plants, and help to save several plant species. In your free time, you can travel to archaeological sites in the area. If you love a **tropical** climate, this is the trip for you.

70

75

80

G   Do you want a very different vacation? Do you want to travel far, work hard, and learn a lot? Then an Earthwatch vacation is for you.

After You Read

7 Finding the Main Idea Read the sentences below. Choose the main idea of "Adventure Vacations."

- (A) A trip with Earthwatch is a good way to learn something and have a vacation, too.
- (B) It's more fun to stay at a hotel than to go camping.
- (C) Disneyland, the Taj Mahal, and the Louvre are wonderful places to see on a vacation.
- (D) Earthwatch trips are difficult.

8 Finding Details Following are the main ideas of Paragraphs A, B, C, and D. Read the details below each main idea. Check (✓) all the details that are in each paragraph.

A: People like different kinds of vacations.

____ Some people go camping.

____ Some people swim, fish, cook over a fire, and sleep outside.

____ Some people stay at a hotel in a city.

____ Some people learn about neighborhood problems.

____ Some people go shopping and dancing.

____ Some people go to special places such as Disneyland.

B: Some people want an adventure.

_____ They want to stay at a hotel and go shopping.

✓_____ They want to learn something and maybe help people, too.

✓_____ Some groups plan special adventures.

✓_____ Earthwatch sends volunteers to different places in the world.

_____ Earthwatch volunteers help in shelters for the homeless.

✓_____ Earthwatch volunteers study the environment, work with animals, and learn about people of the past.

C: Teams of volunteers will study changes to the environment in the Far North.

✓_____ Two teams will study glaciers.

✓_____ The research will occur in Alaska, Canada, and Iceland.

✓_____ One team will study animals and snow.

_____ They will study rivers and lakes.

✓_____ Volunteers will need to be active in cold weather.

D: You can study dolphins in Florida.

_____ Dolphins are a species of fish.

✓_____ Dolphins live in family groups.

✓_____ Dolphins are intelligent.

✓_____ Scientists want to know more about the way that dolphins act with each other.

✓_____ Scientists want to know more about dolphins' health.

_____ Pollution is making dolphins sick.

9 Working with New Words Write the vocabulary words for the meanings below. For help, look back at the boldfaced words in the reading.

Paragraph	Meaning	Vocabulary Word
B	a surprising and exciting trip	adventure
C	fields of ice that move very slowly	glaciers
C	how much of something there is	amount
D	a huge body of water	ocean
F	going away	disappearing

Understanding Words from Their Prefixes

Some parts of words can help you to understand the meaning. Here are three: *pre-*, *archae-*, and *bio-*.

Prefix and Meaning	Example
• *pre-* means "before"	**pre**view = to look at before
• *archae-* means "very old, from the past"	**archae**ology = the study of things from the past
• *bio* means "life"	**bio**logy = the science of living things

10 **Understanding Words from Their Prefixes** Fill in the chart with three words from the reading.

Prefix	Word	Meaning
1. pre-	*prehistory*	= a time before writing
2. archae-	*archaeologist*	= a scientist who studies very old times
3. bio-	*biologist*	= scientists who study living things

FOCUS

Using *go* + verb + *-ing* for Activities

You can use *go* + verb + *-ing* to describe activities that people do for pleasure. Use this structure in the present, past, and future tenses. Also, use it with modals (such as *can*, *should*, or *might*) and verbs such as *like*, *love*, or *hate*.

Examples

We **went hiking** last weekend.

You can **go swimming** in Puerto Vallarta.

I like to **go shopping** if I have money.
(shop)

Here are some common verbs that use this structure:

bowl	dance	hike	sightsee	surf	window-shop
camp	fish	shop	ski	swim	

Culture Note

Working Vacations
Some people "relax" by spending their vacations as volunteers. They work hard during their vacation to help people, but it's different from their usual job, and they enjoy it. What kind of working vacation do you think would be interesting?

11 **Discussing Activities** First, look over the verbs in the list above. Discuss their meanings. For any that you do not know, use a dictionary. Then talk about the activities. Answer the questions below and on the next page.

1. Which of the activities do you like to do? Why?

2. Which activities do you not like to do? Why?

3. When you travel, do you go sightseeing?

4. Did you do any of these activities last week? Last month? Last year?

5. Are you going to do any of these activities next week? Next month? Next year?

PART 2

Main Ideas and Details

Your Travel Personality

Before You Read

1 **Thinking About the Topic** Look at these three photos about different kinds of vacations. Which of the three vacations would *you* like? Write your answer on a piece of paper. Don't tell or show anyone your answer.

I would like to go on vacation to _____.

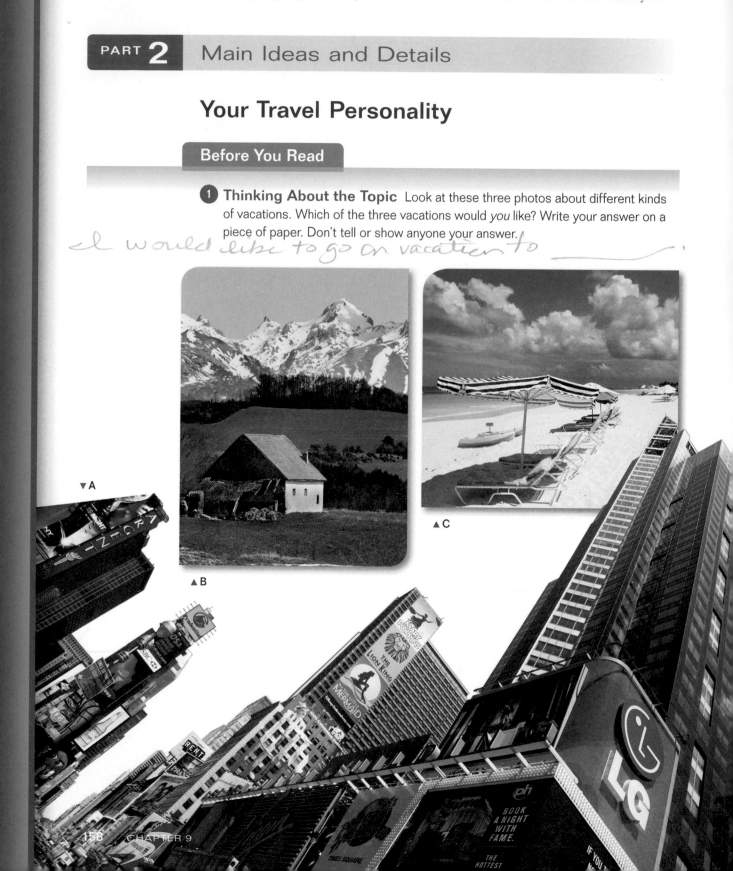

▼A

▲B

▲C

2 **Previewing Vocabulary** Read the words below. Listen to their pronunciation. Do not look them up in a dictionary. Put a check mark (✓) next to the words that you don't know.

Nouns
- campfire
- museum
- personality
- relaxing
- seafood
- water sports
- worries (worry)

Adjective
- boring

Read

3 **Completing a Personality Questionnaire** Read and answer the following questions.

Your Travel Personality

1. What do you like to do in the morning?
   - (A) sleep late
   - (B) exercise
   - (C) watch TV

2. What do you like to do on Saturday and Sunday?
   - (A) go hiking
   - (B) go swimming
   - (C) go shopping

3. What's most interesting to study when you're on vacation?
   - (A) nothing
   - (B) animals
   - (C) paintings in a museum

4. What do you *not* enjoy?
   - (A) a busy, crowded city
   - (B) being cold
   - (C) sleeping outside

5. It's boring to _____.
   - (A) spend the day at the ocean
   - (B) go shopping all day
   - (C) do nothing

6. What gives you a headache?
   - (A) hot weather
   - (B) smoke from buses
   - (C) cold air

7. What's most important?
   - (A) clean water
   - (B) clean air
   - (C) a clean bathroom

8. The best food is _____.
   - (A) cooked over a campfire
   - (B) fresh seafood
   - (C) in a good restaurant

9. I like a vacation to be _____.
   - (A) quiet, with no worries
   - (B) exciting, with adventure
   - (C) exciting, with lots of people

10. Which activity do you like best?
    - (A) relaxing
    - (B) water sports
    - (C) sightseeing

After You Read

Strategy

Reaching a Conclusion: Paying Attention to Evidence
Sometimes a reading gives information but doesn't reach a conclusion—a decision or judgment. As the reader, you need to reach this conclusion *yourself.* Pay attention to the evidence (proof) and make an inference. To do this, "add up" all the details in the reading. Come to a conclusion from these details.

4 **Paying Attention to Evidence** Now exchange books with a partner and read each other's answers to the personality questionnaire. What can you guess about your partner's personality? What picture on page 158 do you think your partner would like? Tell your partner. Does your partner agree with your choice? Next, give your partner suggestions.

Examples "You like cities. Maybe you should go to Hong Kong. It's exciting." OR "Lake Louise is beautiful. You'll like it."

5 **Extending the Lesson: Planning Your Dream Vacation** Form a group with 3–4 people who chose the same vacation photo on page 158. Follow these steps:

1. As a group, make a list of all the places in the world that you would like to visit *on your type* of vacation.

2. Each person does *one* of the following:
   - Go to a travel agency and bring back information on *one* of these places.
   - Find a website with information on *one* of these places.

3. Tell your group what you have learned.

4. As a group, choose one of the places. Plan one perfect day on your "Dream Vacation." Fill in the chart below with that information.

5. Make a report to the class.

Place	Where will you go?	What will you do?	What will you eat?	What will you buy?
Morning				
Afternoon				
Evening				

6 **Writing in Your Journal** Choose one topic below. Write about it for five minutes. Use vocabulary that you learned in this chapter.

- one type of Earthwatch adventure
- your favorite activity
- your idea of the perfect vacation

Tours and Traveling

1 **Reading a Website and Discussing Tours** Look at the photos on the website below and read about the different tours. Then answer the questions that follow.

◄ ► + www.allnews/allday.com

Q Search GO

Q▾ ↻

A. Whale Watching in Mexico

A   The Baja Peninsula of Mexico is one of the best places in the world to see whales. Our experienced sea kayakers and biologists will guide you

and teach you about whale behavior. You don't need kayaking experience, but you should be in good health. 5 Looking into the eye of a whale is an experience you will not forget.

   Length of trip: 12 days
   Group size: 12
   Cost: $3,995   10

B. Maui Bicycling Tour

B   Ride a bicycle around one of the most beautiful tropical islands in the world. Swim in the clear,

▲ Kayaking in Baja

warm, tropical water. Camp in the beautiful national parks. Participants provide and carry camping gear, personal gear, and clothing. We provide the 15 bicycles, food, guides and occasional transportation.

   Length of trip: 8 days
   Group size: 8
   Cost: $680   20

C. French Cooking Tour

C   Do you like French food? Do you like to cook? Visit Paris and seven other French cities. Eat at some of the best restaurants in 25 France. Study cooking with

▲ Bicycling around Maui

some of the most interesting chefs of France. The price includes food and hotel as well as one full week of cooking lessons.

    Length of trip: 8 days   30
    Group sizc: 10
    Cost: $5,800

D. Thailand Jungle Safari

D   This hiking and camping trip provides an adventurous view of the forests and wildlife of western Thailand. 35 We make your trip comfortable with our permanent camps. Spend the days exploring the beautiful forests and exciting animals of Thailand. Spend the nights in our large 40 comfortable sleeping tents. Take a hot shower and eat freshly prepared Thai food after a day of hiking.

    Length of trip: 4 days
    Group size: 14   45
    Cost: $480

▲ Cooking in France

▲ Hiking in the jungle

2 Answering Comprehension Questions Answer the questions about the reading. Discuss your answers with your classmates.

1. Which tour is the most expensive? _____ C Fr. cooking
2. Which tour is the longest? _____ A whale watching in Mex
3. Which tour has the most people? _____ D Thai Jungle Safari
4. Which tour is the most interesting to you? _____
5. Which tour is the least interesting to you? _____

3 Making Connections Now read what different people say about their traveling. Then decide which tour is best for each person. Write the letter of the tour in the blank.

1. _____ C "I love all kinds of food, but I especially love French food. I want to learn to cook it."

2. _____ A "I love adventures! I like to swim, and I want to learn about the ocean."

3. _____ D "I like adventure. I have only four days for my vacation."

4. ___C___ "I'd like to learn something new, and I like Europe."

5. ___D___ "I like nature and I like to hike, but I really want to be comfortable at night."

6. ___B___ "I like to swim and ride my bike. I love to go camping."

PART 4 Vocabulary Practice

1 **Working with Vocabulary** Read these sentences. Check (✓) True or False. New words from this chapter are underlined. When you finish, correct the false sentences.

	True	False
1. An <u>adventure</u> is not usually exciting.	☐	☑
2. <u>Biologists</u> study everything from animals to plants.	☑	☐
3. <u>Pollution</u> is often caused by <u>glaciers</u>.	☐	☑
4. <u>Dolphins</u> are mammals that live in the sea.	☑	☐
5. People don't usually like to feel <u>worried</u> or <u>bored</u>.	☑	☐
6. <u>Archaeologists</u> are often interested in bones.	☑	☐
7. <u>Tropical climates</u> are not usually warm.	☐	☑
8. Climbing trees is an example of some animal <u>behavior</u>.	☑	☐
9. When most people <u>go camping</u>, they stay indoors.	☐	☑
10. People who live on an island probably like <u>seafood</u>.	☑	☐

2 **Listening: Fill in the Missing Words** Listen and fill in the missing words below. Then check your answers on page 154, Paragraph D.

Play audio

Do you enjoy ___ocean___ animals? You can spend two ___weeks___ in Florida. There you can study dolphins. It will be ___exciting___ to learn about these intelligent ocean ___mammals___. These beautiful animals can live to ___over___ 50 years of age. They travel together in family ___groups___. From small boats, volunteers will study and ___photograph___ these groups. The purpose of this ___research___ is to learn about the animals' social behavior.

Scientists want to know what dolphins do and how they live. Also, _scientists_ want to study dolphins' health. For example, they
9
wonder, "Is ocean _pollution_ changing the dolphins' health?" If
10
you like warm _weather_ , the ocean, and animals, this is a good
11
trip for you.
12

3 **Focusing on High-Frequency Words** Read the paragraph below and fill in each blank with a word from the box.

adventure	coast	disappearing	plants
amounts	count	enjoy	travel

Do you _enjoy_ the beach and like to learn about plants?
1
There is an Earthwatch _adventure_ in Yucatan, Mexico. On
2
the north _coast_ of Yucatan, there are beautiful species of
3
plants . Unfortunately, many of them are _disappearing_ .
4   5
People dig them up and sell them for large _amounts_ of money.
6
Mexican biologists need volunteers to collect seeds, _count_
7
plants, and help to save several plant species. In your free time, you can
travel to archaeological sites in the area. If you love a tropical
8
climate, this is the trip for you.

4 **Building Vocabulary** Complete the crossword puzzle on the next page. This puzzle uses words from Chapters 8 and 9.

adventure	climate	pollution	species
amount	intelligent	prefer	spend
attractive	irony	raw	together
behavior	obesity	slim	tropical
bored	overweight	southwest	

Across

1. examples: smoke in the air, garbage in the water (n.)
6. a group of living things (n.)
8. how much there is of something (n.)
9. opposite of *ugly* (adj.)
13. the opposite of what we expected (n.)
14. opposite of *fat* (adj.)
16. to like something more than something else (v.)
18. weighing more than average or normal (adj.)
19. a trip that isn't boring at all (n.)

Down

2. condition of very heavy people (n.)
3. We do this with time and money. (v.)
4. the way we act (n.)
5. You're in eastern Canada. Which direction is Mexico? (adj.)
7. smart, like dolphins, for example (adj.)
10. examples: temperature, rain, wind (n.)
11. opposite of *apart* (adj.)
12. Palm trees, warm weather, and rain forests are in _____ climates. (adj.)
15. not cooked (adj)
17. not interested (adj.)

Key: *adj.* = adjective; *adv.* = adverb; *n.* = noun; *prep.* = preposition; *v.* = verb

Self-Assessment Log

Read the lists below. Check (✓) the strategies and vocabulary that you learned in this chapter. Look through the chapter or ask your instructor about the strategies and words that you do not understand.

Reading and Vocabulary-Building Strategies

☐ Understanding words for direction
☐ Finding the main idea
☐ Finding details
☐ Understanding words from their prefixes
☐ Using *go* + verb + *-ing* for activities
☐ Reaching a conclusion: paying attention to evidence
☐ Reading a website

Target Vocabulary

Nouns

- adventure
- amount*
- archaeologists
- behavior
- biologists
- campfire
- climate
- coast*
- dolphins
- glaciers

- museum
- ocean*
- personality
- plants*
- pollution
- prehistory
- relaxing
- seafood
- seeds*
- species

- water* sports
- worries (worry)
- weather*

Verbs

- count*
- disappearing
- go* camping
- go* sightseeing
- prefer
- travel*

Adjectives

- bored
- boring
- intelligent
- tropical
- worried

Adverb

- together*

*These words are among the 1,000 most-frequently used words in English.

10 Our Planet

The survival of the world depends upon our
sharing what we have and working together.
If we don't, the whole world will die. First
the planet, and next the people.

Frank Fools Crow
Ceremonial Chief of the Native American nation, Teton Sioux

In this
CHAPTER

In Part 1, you will read about environmental problems in the ocean. In the rest of this chapter, you will read about, discuss, and explore things we do to harm our environment, and things we can do to help save it.

Connecting to the Topic

1. What do you see in this photo? What do you think the men are doing?

2. Why is it important to plant trees?

3. Name five things that you think are harmful to the planet. Name five things you think are helpful.

The Ocean in Trouble

Before You Read

1 **Thinking About the Topic** Look at the photos and answer the questions.

1. Describe each photo. What do you see?

2. Which countries have a lot of coastline, lakes, and rivers? Do you think fishing is important in those places?

3. Do you eat a lot of seafood? Do you think people eat more seafood now than they ate in the past? If so, why?

4. Do you know of any problems for the fishing industry?

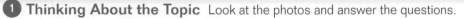
▼ Seafood for restaurants

◄ Commercial fishing trawler with its nets

▼ Fishing nets

Fishers repairing their nets. ►

2 Previewing Vocabulary Read the words below. Listen to their pronunciation. Do not look them up in a dictionary. Put a check mark (✓) next to the words that you don't know.

Nouns

- amount
- areas
- crabs
- damage
- danger
- dolphins
- environmentalists
- methods
- nets

- overfishing
- trawlers
- whales
- zones

Verbs

- catch
- create
- destroy

- drag
- influence
- police
- pressure
- prove
- reproduce
- urged
- warning

Adjectives

- extinct
- fake

Adverb

- only

Preposition

- but

3 Finding the Meaning of New Words Find the meanings of the underlined words. Look at the sentence or phrase before or after the word for help.

1. George loves to eat, and he likes all kinds of food. He'll eat anything <u>but</u> insects because he thinks they're disgusting.

   (A) however

   (B) except for

   (C) and

2. The large boat <u>dragged</u> another small boat behind it through the water.

   (A) pulled

   (B) pushed

   (C) repaired

3. Our great-grandparents sometimes saw that species, but now we can't because it's <u>extinct</u>, like the dinosaurs.

   (A) hard to find

   (B) completely dead

   (C) only in zoos

4. After the people of the city <u>pressured</u> the government, the government built a new road.

   (A) caused worry to

   (B) strongly influenced

   (C) emailed

5. At first, the biologists made suggestions. The government didn't do anything about the problem, however, so now the biologists are <u>urging</u> the government to do something.

   (A) doing more research

   (B) hoping

   (C) strongly asking

6. "If you eat that, you'll get sick," he <u>warned</u> me.

(A) predicted something bad

(B) asked

(C) showed

Read

4 **Reading an Article** Read the following article. Don't use your dictionary. If you don't know some words, try to figure out their meanings. Then do the activities.

The Ocean in Trouble

A   Many environmental groups are **warning** that oceans worldwide are in great **danger**. According to the United Nations Food and Agriculture Organization (FAO), 70 percent of the world's fishing areas are in danger. One reason, of course, is the huge **amount** of pollution. However, there is another danger, and it might be even more harmful than pollution. 5 This danger is **overfishing**. "No matter where you look in the world, on average, 90 percent of the fish are gone," says a biologist from Dalhousie University in Canada.

New Technology

B   Fishers are finding fewer and fewer fish everywhere. However, this does not mean that fishermen are not fishing any longer. Instead, many 10 are using new technology to fish new waters as deep as a mile. Trawlers (large fishing boats) are using special **nets** on wheels and rollers. They **drag** these nets across the bottom of the deep oceans, and they pick up anything of any size at all. With these nets, fishers **catch** the fish that people eat, but the nets also catch marine mammals such as sea lions, 15 dolphins, and sometimes **whales**.

The Effect on Fish

C   These nets also take species like squid, skate, red **crabs**, slackjaw eels, spiny dogfish, and orange roughy. A few years ago, people didn't want to eat these species. Now you can find them in fish stores, in fish sandwiches at fast-food restaurants, or in **fake**—not real—"crab meat" for seafood salads. 20 The orange roughy provides an example of what is happening. This fish appeared in fish stores **only** about ten years ago, but already the species is almost **extinct**. The orange roughy lives very deep in the ocean—up to a mile deep—in the cold waters off New Zealand. Scientists now know that fish in deep cold water grow and **reproduce** very slowly. For example, the 25 orange roughy lives to be 150 years old. It doesn't start to reproduce until it is 30 years old. Although the fish is nearly extinct, people still sell it in seafood stores and in restaurants. And, of course, it may be in that fish sandwich that you eat at a fast-food restaurant.

D   Many scientists believe that present fishing **methods** will **destroy** all the large fishing areas of the world. Can anything stop this? Some scientists think that governments should stop the fishing industry from using some kinds of technology. But this will be difficult. Many of the big fishing companies have a lot of money, and they use that money to **influence** politicians all around the world.

▲ Crab is more expensive than other seafood, so the "crab" in your crab salad might be fake.

No Fishing Zones

E   Other scientists believe that governments should **create** no-fishing **zones**—areas where no one can fish. Governments can **police** these areas. During the U.N. International Year of the Ocean, more than 1,600 leading marine scientists and conservation biologists from 65 countries **urged** the world to create 80 times the no-fishing areas that exist now. Their goal is to protect 20 percent of the world's oceans by the year 2020. This is happening in some places; for example, the fishing industry in Britain is beginning to accept no-fishing zones because the amount of fish that the industry catches is getting smaller and smaller.

F   The fishing industry often argues that the scientific evidence is not complete—that we just don't know what is going on in the oceans. Now, scientists and **environmentalists** have to give evidence to show that the fishing industry is doing **damage** before the government will pass laws protecting the ocean. This takes time, and sometimes it is difficult to **prove** something like this. The magazine *Science* says we should have the opposite rule: big fishing companies should have to prove that they are *not* destroying the oceans before we allow them to fish.

Conclusion

G   Environmentalists say that average people need to get together and **pressure** their governments to do something. The large fishing companies that own the big trawlers are not going to stop fishing by themselves. The environmentalists say that if we don't pressure our governments, there will be nothing left in the oceans **but** water.

5 **Reaching a Conclusion** Come to a conclusion about the writer's purpose in "The Ocean in Trouble." Why did he write this? Choose the correct answer below.

(A) to give the reader information about why the fishing industry is important

(B) to help the reader understand how the fishing industry works and also understand about deep water fish like the orange roughy

(C) to tell the reader about the problems caused by overfishing and suggest possible solutions

(D) to tell the reader about the problems of ocean pollution

6 **Finding the Main Idea** The main idea of the reading is that _____

New fishing tech's are causing damage to the oceans, + smthg needs 2 b dn abt it.

7 **Working with New Words** Write the vocabulary words for the meanings below. For help, look back at the boldfaced words in the reading.

Paragraph	Meaning	Word
C	have babies	reproduce
E	areas	zones
F	people who work to take care of the environment	environmentalists
F	give evidence to show that something is true	prove

Strategy

Understanding Words from Their Parts: *Over* in a Word
Some parts of words can help you to understand the meaning of the word. *Over* is such a word. At the beginning of a word, *over* can mean "too much" or "more than is good."

Example
One great danger to oceans worldwide is **overfishing**.
(You see that *overfishing* means "taking too many fish from the ocean.")

8 Understanding Words from their Parts Can you figure out a word for each blank below? Use *over* in each word. Follow the example.

1. If you did too much and got tired, you ____*overdid*____ it.

2. If you eat too much, you might get sick because it's not good to
   _____overeat_____.

3. It's not a good idea to work too much. Please try not to _____overwork_____.

4. If you sleep too late, you will be late for work. Set your alarm clock so you don't
   _____oversleep_____.

5. If you spend too much money on clothes, you might not have enough for food.
   It's a good idea to have a budget so that you don't _____overspend_____.

FOCUS

Understanding Words That Can Be More Than One Part of Speech

Many words in English can be more than one part of speech. For example, a word might be both a noun and a verb. Often, the meaning is similar. Sometimes it's different.

Examples

There aren't enough **police** in this city.
  (In this sentence, *police* is a noun. It means *people whose job is protecting the public*.)

Governments have to **police** the oceans.
  (Here, *police* is a verb. It means *to keep order in a place*.)

---

9 Understanding Words That Can Be More Than One Part of Speech What is the part of speech of each underlined word—noun or verb?

	Part of Speech
1. They shouldn't <u>fish</u> in that area.	V
2. I eat <u>fish</u> several times a week.	n
3. In the future, there might be nothing in the ocean but <u>water</u>.	n
4. In hot weather, you need to <u>water</u> the garden every day.	V
5. They don't usually <u>catch</u> many fish anymore.	V
6. Their <u>catch</u> of fish was good this week.	n
7. There is a lot of <u>pressure</u> on the fishing industry.	n
8. Environmental groups often <u>pressure</u> the fishing industry to do things differently.	V

Strategy

Understanding Relationships Between Ideas

Understanding the relationship between ideas and details in a reading is important.
You can use graphic organizers or charts to help. Some are simple. Others are more
complicated. They can help you to "see" ideas. If you put information from a reading
on a graphic organizer, it can help you to study for exams. You will pratice using a
graphic organizer below.

Purpose?

10 Understanding Relationships Between Ideas Below is a graphic
organizer about "The Ocean in Trouble." Look back at the reading on pages
172–173 and fill in the missing information.

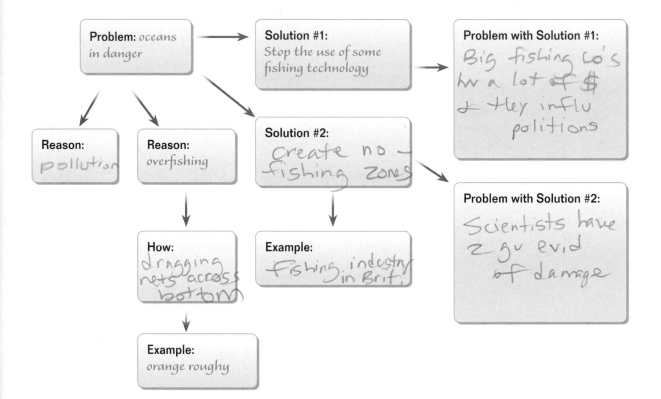

Problem: *oceans in danger*

Solution #1: *Stop the use of some fishing technology*

Problem with Solution #1: Big fishing co's hv a lot of $ & they influ politions

Reason: pollution

Reason: *overfishing*

Solution #2: create no fishing zones

Problem with Solution #2: Scientists have z gv evid of damage

How: dragging nets across bottom

Example: Fishing industry in Brit.

Example: *orange roughy*

11 Discussing the Reading Discuss your answers to the following questions.

1. What solution to the problem of overfishing does the writer give at the end of
the article? In your opinion, is this a good idea? Why or why not?

2. The writer writes about two groups—the fishing industry and
environmentalists. Which group does the writer agree with? Why do you think
this? (Find evidence for your answer in the reading.)

Repairing the Environment

Before You Read

1 **Interviewing** Read the two questions in the chart below. Write your own question about the environment. Decide on your answers. Then walk around the room and ask three students these questions. Write their answers in the chart.

Questions	Student 1	Student 2	Student 3
1. What are problems with the environment in your city, state, province, or country?			
2. What prediction can you make about the environment 50 years in the future?			
3. *(Your question)* Is there something indiv. or groups can do to help the environment now? What?			

2 **Previewing Vocabulary** Read the words below. Listen to their pronunciation. Do not look them up in a dictionary. Put a check mark (✓) next to the words that you don't know.

Nouns
- canoes
- cloth bag
- containers
- damage
- garbage
- island
- plastic bags
- statues
- stone
- trash
- vegetation

Verbs
- absorb
- arrived
- build
- cut down
- last
- melting
- mention
- produce
- recycle
- stopped

Adjectives
- amazing
- ancient
- organic
- plastic
- surrounding

3 **Reading an Article** Read this article. Then do the activities that follow.

Repairing the Environment

Early Life on Easter Island

A   Easter Island is a very small **island** in the Pacific Ocean. In the **ancient** past, the island was covered with **vegetation**, such as beautiful forests, and the **surrounding** ocean was rich in fish. The human population grew to about 9,000 people. Today, we know them for their art—hundreds of huge, **amazing statues** that are made of **stone**. Over several hundred years, the   5 people created larger and larger statues.

The Changing History

B   For about 700 years, life on Easter Island was good. However, by the 16th century, people suddenly **stopped** creating the statues. Also, the environment completely changed. The earth didn't **produce** enough   10 food for the population. The forests were gone because people **cut down** all the trees. Without trees, they couldn't even **build canoes**—a kind   15 of small boat—and for this reason, they couldn't go fishing. The society was destroyed. The people were hungry. When Europeans   20 **arrived** in 1722, there were only about 2,000 people left.

▲ At one time, Easter Island was covered with vegetation and forests.
The people created amazing stone statues.

Easter Island as an Example

C   Scientists often **mention** Easter Island. They see it as an example of the **damage** that humans can do to the environment. They say that our Earth is like an island. When we destroy it, we destroy ourselves. They say that   25 we are now destroying it. Like the people of ancient Easter Island, we are cutting down forests. Worldwide, the environment is changing. The climate is becoming warmer. Glaciers are **melting**. Pollution fills many rivers and lakes and the air of many cities. And every year, about 20,000 plant and animal species become extinct.   30

What We Can Do

D   Some people see this situation as hopeless, but environmentalists say that it isn't too late. There *are* things that we can do. Governments and big companies need to make big changes, but every individual can make many small changes. All these small changes can add up. They can make a big difference. Here are just some:

▲ Paper, plastic, or cloth?

35

- Plant trees. Trees **absorb** ("drink in") the carbon dioxide (CO_2) that factories put into the air. 40

- Buy **organic** fruits and vegetables— ones without dangerous chemicals. These are good for your health and good for the Earth, too. 45

- Reuse **containers**; in other words, don't throw empty **plastic** food containers into the **trash** or **garbage**. Wash them and use them again. Also, use **plastic bags** many 50 times. When you throw away a plastic bag or container, it stays in the earth for *thousands of years*.

- Don't use paper or plastic bags. Bring a **cloth bag** with you to the supermarket. You can use the same cloth 55 bag over and over for years.

▲ A regular light bulb

▲ A compact fluorescent light bulb

- **Recycle** things that you can't reuse. You can recycle aluminum cans, glass bottles, some plastic containers, and newspapers.

- Use compact fluorescent light bulbs. They **last** ten times longer than regular light bulbs, so they save you money. Also, they use 75 percent less 60 energy. One of these bulbs can keep 1/2 ton (1,000 pounds) of carbon dioxide out of the air.

- Do you eat tuna fish? If so, look carefully at the can. Buy only tuna 65 that is dolphin-safe—in other words, tuna from companies with special nets that don't kill dolphins.

◄ Is your tuna fish dolphin-safe?

- Write letters to government leaders. Ask them for laws that protect the environment. Tell them that you want the 70 Earth to be here for your great-great grandchildren.

4 Finding the Main Idea Read the sentences below. Which one is the main idea of "Repairing the Environment"?

Ⓐ In the past, Easter Island had a beautiful environment, but the people destroyed it when they cut down all the trees.

Ⓑ There are things that individual people can do to help the environment.

Ⓒ Some environmentalists think that the situation is hopeless, but others say that it's not too late to save the Earth.

Ⓓ If we make some changes in the way that we live, we don't have to repeat the mistake of the people of Easter Island, who destroyed their environment.

5 Working with New Words Write the vocabulary words for the meanings below. For help, look back at the boldfaced words in the reading.

Paragraph	Meaning	Word
A	a type of art	
B	a type of small boat	
C	changing from ice to water	
D	drink in	
D	use something again; reuse	

6 Finding Details Look back at Paragraphs B and C on page 178 for the answers to these questions.

1. Why couldn't the people of Easter Island go fishing? *couldn't build canoes*

2. Why couldn't they build canoes? *There were no trees*

3. What is happening to the Earth's environment today? *We are cutting down forests. Climate warmer. Glaciers melting. Pollution fills many rivers, lakes, air. Plants & animals becoming extinct*

7 Discussing the Reading Discuss your answers to the following questions.

1. Look at the list in Paragraph D of the reading. Do you do any of those things? If so, which ones? Are there other things that you do?

2. What's good about organic fruits and vegetables? Can you think of a possible problem with them? *Are not grown w/ pesticides, so better for ppl & environ. Are more expensive.*

3. Does your city have a recycling program? If so, talk about it with your group.

8 Writing in Your Journal Choose one topic below. Write about it for five minutes. Use vocabulary that you learned in this chapter.

- something that you learned about the ocean
- something that you learned about Easter Island
- your ideas on ways to help the environment

Using Facts and Figures

1 **Reading a Graph** The graph below tells how many pounds of garbage a person makes on each day in eleven cities. Look at the graph and answer the questions.

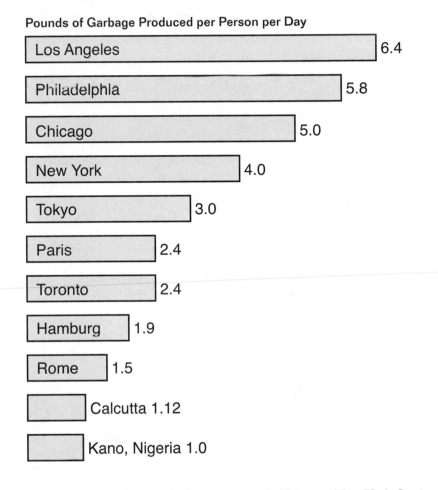

Pounds of Garbage Produced per Person per Day

Los Angeles	6.4
Philadelphia	5.8
Chicago	5.0
New York	4.0
Tokyo	3.0
Paris	2.4
Toronto	2.4
Hamburg	1.9
Rome	1.5
Calcutta 1.12
Kano, Nigeria 1.0

1. Who makes more garbage each day—a person in Tokyo or New York City?

   _____NYC_____

2. Who makes more garbage each day—a person in Toronto or Los Angeles?

   _____LA_____

3. Who makes more garbage each day—a person in Calcutta or Paris?

   _____Paris_____

Comparing Facts and Figures in a Graph Choose the best answer to complete the sentences.

1. Five people in Kano, Nigeria, make the same amount of garbage each day as

   _____.

   Ⓐ two people in Rome
   Ⓑ one person in Chicago
   Ⓒ two people in Toronto

2. Five people in Calcutta, India, make about the same amount of garbage as

   _____.

   Ⓐ three people in Los Angeles
   Ⓑ two people in Chicago
   Ⓒ one person in Philadelphia

FYI

Note: 16 oz. = 1
pound = .45 kilos

3 Reading a Paragraph with a Chart Read about Kenji and Tanya. Then answer the questions. Refer to the graph on page 181.

> Kenji recycles his metal cans. He takes them to a recycling center so they can be used again. He doesn't throw any in the garbage. He recycles his paper products. He puts his yard waste in a pile and puts it on his garden later. Here is a list of what he put in the garbage today.
>
> | | |
> |---|---|
> | metal cans | 0 oz. |
> | food waste | 8 oz. |
> | yard waste | 0 oz. |
> | paper products | 0 oz. |
> | glass bottles, jars, etc. | 16 oz. |

1. How much garbage did Kenji throw away? __24 oz__
2. That is the average for what city? __Rome__

> Tanya likes to read the newspaper and work in the yard. Sometimes she recycles and sometimes she doesn't. Tanya throws out a lot of things. Today she threw out the following things.
>
> | | |
> |---|---|
> | bottles | 14 oz. |
> | soda cans and tin cans | 8 oz. |
> | one newspaper, some letters, a magazine | 30 oz. |
> | extra food | 12 oz. |
> | yard waste | 16 oz. |

1. How many pounds of garbage did Tanya throw out? (Hint: Add the total ounces, then divide by 16.)

5 lbs

2. Tanya's garbage was exactly average for her city. Where does Tanya live?

Chicago

> How about you? What did you throw out or recycle yesterday? Make a list.
>
> | _Throw out_ | _Recycle_ |
> |---|---|
> | _plastic wrappers_ | _plastic bottles\caps_ |
> | _old or scraps food_ | _juice/milk cartons_ |
> | _tissues, paper_ | _newspapers/cardboard_ |

4 **Reading a Pie Chart** Garbage is created all over the world every day. Look at this pie chart about garbage in the U.S. Answer the questions below and on page 184.

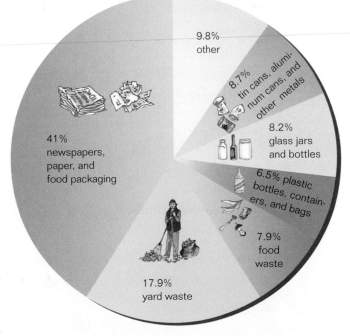

9.8% other

8.7% tin cans, aluminum cans, and other metals

8.2% glass jars and bottles

6.5% plastic bottles, containers, and bags

7.9% food waste

17.9% yard waste

41% newspapers, paper, and food packaging

▲ Breakdown of garbage in the U.S.

1. In the U.S. is there a larger percentage of newspapers or plastic bottles?

There is a larger percentage of newspapers.

2. What percentage is larger: yard waste or metal cans?

3. What percentage is greater: glass or plastic bottles?

_____

4. What percentage of the trash are metal cans and other metals?

8.7

_____

5. What percentage of the trash are grass clippings and other yard waste?

17.9

_____

6. What percentage of the trash is food waste?

7.9

_____

PART **4**   Vocabulary Practice

1 **Building Vocabulary** Match the words and phrases that go together.

1. __h__ dolphins   a. "Be careful!"
2. __f__ catch   b. zones
3. __d__ extinct   c. have babies
4. __j__ amount   d. gone from the Earth
5. __e__ ancient   e. very old
6. __b__ areas   f. fish in a net
7. __g__ pressure   g. influence
8. __a__ warning   h. mammals
9. __i__ wheels   i. rollers
10. __c__ reproduce   j. percentage

2 **Using Your Vocabulary** Write new sentences using the words next to each number. You can look at the readings in Parts 1 and 2 if you need help.

1. warn / scientists / oceans

   Scientists warned us that the oceans are in trouble.

2. extinct / species

   _____

3. money / influence / government

   _____

4. methods / destroy / fishing areas

   _____

5. pollution / overfishing / oceans

_____

6. environmentalists / damage / prove

_____

7. Easter Island / trees

_____

8. reproduce / cold water / slowly

_____

9. canoes / fishing

_____

 3 **Listening: Focusing on High-Frequency Words** Listen and fill in the blanks in the sentences.

For about 700 years, life on Easter Island was good. However, by the 16ᵗʰ century, people suddenly ___stopped___ creating the statues. Also, the environment completely changed. The earth didn't ___produce___ enough food for the ___population___. The forests were gone because people ___cut down___ all the trees. Without trees, they couldn't even ___build___ canoes—a kind of small boat—and for this reason, they couldn't go ___fishing___. The society was destroyed. The people were hungry. When Europeans ___arrived___ in 1722, there were ___only___ about 2,000 people left.

4 **Building Vocabulary** Complete the crossword puzzle. This puzzle uses words from Chapters 9 and 10.

ancient	climate	influence	ocean	pressure	seed	urge
behavior	extinct	island	overfish	prove	statue	warn
bored	fake	nets	pollution	reproduce	stone	zone

Across

2. example: weather that is cold in winter, warm in summer (n.)
4. examples: eating, communicating, fighting, reproducing (n.)
6. junk that people put in the air, sea, etc. (n.)
8. Lawyers have to _____ that a criminal is guilty. (v.)
11. Ancient people used tools made of this. (n.)
12. very old, in the far past (adj.)
14. things used to catch butterflies or fish (n.)
16. ask someone strongly (v.)
17. have babies (v.)
18. area made for a special purpose (n.)
19. not alive anywhere on the Earth anymore (adj.)

Down

1. A plant begins from this. (n.)
3. land surrounded by water (n.)
5. use power over someone or something (v.)
7. not real (adj.)
8. strongly influence someone to do something (v.)
9. example: Pacific, Atlantic (n.)
10. opposite of excited (adj.)
11. example: a huge sculpture, found on Easter Island (n.)
13. catch too many fish (v.)
15. tell someone about danger (v.)

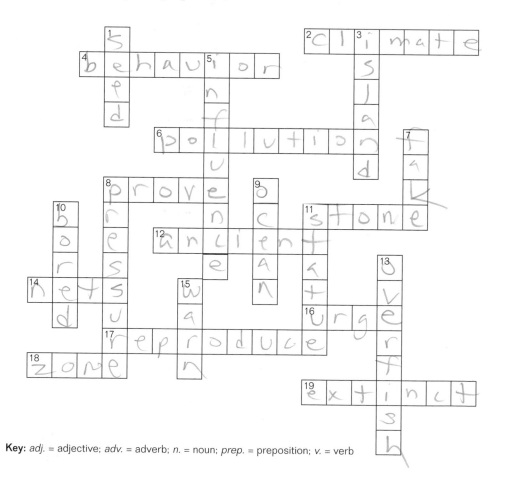

Key: *adj.* = adjective; *adv.* = adverb; *n.* = noun; *prep.* = preposition; *v.* = verb

Self-Assessment Log

Read the lists below. Check (✓) the strategies and vocabulary that you learned in this chapter. Look through the chapter or ask your instructor about the strategies and words that you do not understand.

Reading and Vocabulary-Building Strategies

- ☐ Finding the meaning of words from context
- ☐ Making inferences
- ☐ Finding the main idea
- ☐ Understanding words from their parts: *over* in a word
- ☐ Understanding words that can be more than one part of speech
- ☐ Understanding relationships between ideas
- ☐ Finding details
- ☐ Reading a graph
- ☐ Comparing facts and figures in a graph
- ☐ Reading a paragraph with a chart
- ☐ Reading a pie chart

Target Vocabulary

Nouns
- amount*
- areas*
- canoes
- cloth bags
- containers
- crabs
- damage
- danger
- dolphins
- environmentalists
- garbage
- island*

- methods
- nets
- overfishing
- plastic bags
- statues
- stone*
- trash
- trawlers
- vegetation
- whales
- zones

Verbs
- absorb
- arrived*
- build*
- catch*
- create*
- cut* down*
- destroy
- drag
- influence
- last
- melting

- mention
- police

Adjectives
- extinct
- fake

Adverb
- only*

Preposition
- but*

* These words are among the 1,000 most-frequently used words in English.

Vocabulary Index

*These words are among the 1,000 most frequently used words in English

nose
often*
overweight
physical
pounds*
seldom
should*
shoulder*
sleep*
sleep-deprived
small intestine
smoke
solves
sometimes*
stomach
stress
surprising
throat
thumb
toes
university
usually*
wrinkles
wrist

Chapter 5

active
argue
body* language*
comfortable
communicate
connect
equal*/equality
eye* contact
fields*
funny
genders
hierarchy
nod
participate/participation
personal
position*
similar*
status
suggestions

Chapter 6

anxious
awake
childhood
complicated
desires
emotions
evidence
familiar
Freud
hormone
however*
logic
make* sense*
occurs
outside*
predict
psychologists
purpose
realized
repair
research
stage
symbols*
theories (theory)
traveling*
unfamiliar
vision
wonder*

Chapter 7

AIDS
contrast
crime
daily
delivering
drugs
email
energy*
environment
famous*
fun*
hardships
homeless
homelessness
lives* (life) *
lonely

mammals
planted*
prepare*
release
street* children*
take* care* of*
taught (teach)
teenagers
tough
volunteer
world*

Chapter 8

attractive
bake
boil
bugs
calories (calorie)
centers*
dairy
delicious
diabetes
disgusting
entomologists
except*
fried
fry
gain
insects*
irony
join*
lose
marinate
obesity
people*
protein
raw
slim
snacks
spend
thousands*
ugly
while*
worldwide

Chapter 9

adventure
amount*
archaeologists
behavior
biologists
bored
boring
campfire
climate
coast*
count*
disappearing
  (disappear)
dolphins
glaciers
go* camping
go* sightseeing
intelligent
museum
ocean*
personality
plants*
pollution
prefer
prehistory
relaxing
seafood
seeds*
species
together*
travel*
tropical
water* sports
weather*
worried
worries (worry)

Chapter 10

absorb
amount*
areas*
arrived*
build*
but*
canoes
catch*
cloth bags
containers
crabs
create*
cut* down*
damage
danger
destroy
dolphins
drag
environmentalists
extinct
fake
garbage
influence
island*
last*
melting
mention
methods*
nets
only*
overfishing
plastic bags
police
pressure
produce*
prove
recycle
reproduce

statues
stone*
stopped*
trash
trawlers
urged
vegetation
warning
whales
zones

*These words are among the 1,000 most frequently used words in English

Populations of U.S. Universities and Their Cities

University	City	Population of the City (2010)	Population of the University (2010–2011)
New York University	Manhattan, New York		43,404
Arizona State University	Tempe, Arizona	161,719	
The University of Southern California	Los Angeles, California		34,828
The University of Central Florida	Orlando, Florida		56,235
Boston University	Boston, Massachusetts	617,594	
DePaul University	Chicago, Illinois	2,695,598	
George Washington University	Washington, D.C.		25,061

Sources: 1) US Census Bureau websites for individual cities; 2) infoplease.com; 3) http://en.wikipedia.org/wiki/List_of_United_States_university_campuses_by_enrollment

Populations of U.S. Universities and Their Cities

University	City	Population of the City (2010)	Population of the University (2010–2011)
New York University	Manhattan, New York	1,634,795	
Arizona State University	Tempe, Arizona		58,371
The University of Southern California	Los Angeles, California	3,792,621	
The University of Central Florida	Orlando, Florida	238,300	
Boston University	Boston, Massachusetts		31,960
DePaul University	Chicago, Illinois		25,072
George Washington University	Washington, D.C.	601,723	

Sources: 1) US Census Bureau websites for individual cities; 2) infoplease.com; 3) http://en.wikipedia .org/wiki/List_of_United_States_university_campuses_by_enrollment

Skills Index